Instant Colour

Alan
Titchmarsh
how to garden

Instant
Colour

BOOKS

10 9 8 7 6 5 4 3 2 1

Published in 2012 by BBC Books, an imprint of
Ebury Publishing, a Random House Group Company

The Random House Group Limited
supports the Forest Stewardship
Council® (FSC®), the leading
international forest certification
organisation. All our titles that are
printed on Greenpeace approved
FSC® certified paper carry the
FSC® logo. Our paper procurement
policy can be found at www.
rbooks.co.uk/environment

FSC
www.fsc.org
MIX
Paper from
responsible sources
FSC™ C004592

A CIP catalogue record for this book is available from
the British Library.

ISBN 978 1 84 990219 9

Produced by OutHouse!
Shalbourne, Marlborough, Wiltshire SN8 3QJ

BBC BOOKS
COMMISSIONING EDITOR: Lorna Russell
PROJECT EDITOR: Caroline McArthur
PRODUCTION: Rebecca Jones

OUTHOUSE!
COMMISSIONING EDITOR: Sue Gordon
SERIES EDITOR & PROJECT EDITOR: Polly Boyd
SERIES ART DIRECTOR: Robin Whitecross
CONTRIBUTING EDITOR: Jo Weeks
DESIGNERS: Heather McCarry, Louise Turpin
ILLUSTRATIONS by Lizzie Harper, Susan Hillier,
Janet Tanner
PHOTOGRAPHS by Jonathan Buckley except where
credited otherwise on page 96
CONCEPT DEVELOPMENT & SERIES DESIGN:
Elizabeth Mallard-Shaw, Sharon Cluett

Colour origination by Altaimage, London
Printed and bound by Firmengruppe APPL,
Wemding, Germany

Contents

Introduction

Gardening is one of the best and most fulfilling activities on earth, but it can sometimes seem complicated and confusing. The answers to problems can usually be found in books, but big fat gardening books can be rather daunting. Where do you start? How can you find just the information you want without wading through lots of stuff that is not appropriate to your particular problem? Well, a good index is helpful, but sometimes a smaller book devoted to one particular subject fits the bill better – especially if it is reasonably priced and if you have a small garden where you might not be able to fit in everything suggested in a larger volume.

The *How to Garden* books aim to fill that gap – even if sometimes it may be only a small one. They are clearly set out and written, I hope, in a straightforward, easy-to-understand style. I don't see any point in making gardening complicated, when much of it is based on common sense and observation. (All the key techniques are explained and illustrated, and I've included plenty of tips and tricks of the trade.)

There are suggestions on the best plants and the best varieties to grow in particular situations and for a particular effect. I've tried to keep the information crisp and to the point so that you can find what you need quickly and easily and then put your new-found knowledge into practice. Don't worry if you're not familiar with the Latin names of plants. They are there to make sure you can find the plant as it will be labelled in the nursery or garden centre, but where appropriate I have included common names, too. Forgetting a plant's name need not stand in your way when it comes to being able to grow it.

Above all, the *How to Garden* books are designed to fill you with passion and enthusiasm for your garden and all that its creation and care entails, from designing and planting it to maintaining it and enjoying it. For more than fifty years gardening has been my passion, and that initial enthusiasm for watching plants grow, for trying something new and for just being outside pottering has never faded. If anything I am keener on gardening now than I ever was and get more satisfaction from my plants every day. It's not that I am simply a romantic, but rather that I have learned to look for the good in gardens and in plants, and there is lots to be found. Oh, there are times when I fail – when my plants don't grow as well as they should and I need to try harder. But where would I rather be on a sunny day? Nowhere!

The *How to Garden* handbooks will, I hope, allow some of that enthusiasm – childish though it may be – to rub off on you, and the information they contain will, I hope, make you a better gardener, as well as opening your eyes to the magic of plants and flowers.

Introducing bedding plants

There is nothing like bedding plants for adding instant colour to your garden. 'Bedding' is a general term for a very varied bunch of plants with two things in common: they are usually temporary residents and most make an immediate impact. Whether you're wanting to add splashes of colour to flower beds, mixed borders or paved areas, there are always plenty of bedding plants to fit the bill. And what's more, you can ring the changes every year by choosing different colour schemes.

What are bedding plants?

Traditionally, the term 'bedding plant' is associated with annuals and biennials, but the range of plants grown under this banner increases year by year and today also includes perennials (usually tender), bulbs, small shrubs and even miniature trees, such as conifers. Generally, colourful bedding plants are arranged in extravagant displays near the entrance of garden centres. They are put there deliberately to tempt you, just as sweets are placed beside checkouts at supermarkets.

Perennials can be used for short-term, seasonal displays, such as this purple heuchera in a large tea cup.

Using bedding

The great thing about bedding plants is that they're so versatile. You can add them to existing beds and borders to provide much-needed colour when flowers are scarce in the garden – for instance, in autumn and winter or in late summer – or to fill gaps, perhaps where newly planted shrubs and perennials have not yet grown into their allotted space. In addition, you can devote whole flower beds to these brightly coloured plants, changing them with the seasons for eye-catching, high-impact displays. Finally, bedding plants are ideal for pots, window boxes and hanging baskets, making it possible to grow them just about anywhere, even if you don't have a garden.

All bedding plants are suitable for adding colour and most are easy to grow and look after. However, their uses and requirements vary in a number of ways depending on the type of plant they are. It is useful to understand their differences so that you get the best from them.

Annuals

Annuals are plants that grow very quickly from seed and can be in flower within a couple of months from sowing. They usually start growing in spring and are dead by autumn, so their main ambition is to flower and set seed in this time to ensure their survival.

Along with tender perennials, annuals are the mainstay of summer bedding and one of the fastest ways to introduce colour into your garden. They include well-known plants such as lobelia, petunias and tobacco plants (*Nicotiana*), but there are many others in different shades,

Combinations of annuals make a huge impact in pots on the patio. Here, the flowers of red and pink petunias are set off by the tall, purple pennisetum grass.

The subtle colours in this spring border are provided by the tall tulip 'Bleu Aimable' with a foreground of mauve wallflowers and lavender-coloured violas.

flowering stage because they aren't particularly decorative in the garden before then. Many can be raised in containers and potted up as they grow bigger, but some, including wallflowers, are best in nursery beds. All this means that it is usually easier to buy them as plants; wallflowers are often sold very inexpensively in bare-rooted bundles in the autumn. Most potted biennials grow best if planted into their flowering positions soon after purchase to allow them to put down roots and do some final maturing before blooming.

Bulbs

Bulbs are perennial, which means that they live for many years. The most common ones, including daffodils (*Narcissus*), are hardy, so can survive outside through winter. Many varieties are invaluable for early colour and cheer and can be planted in autumn for a wonderful display the following year without any further care. Although hardy, tulips are frequently dug up after flowering, partly because they tend not to flower as well in subsequent years. Other hardy bulbs can be left in place, depending on your plans for your flower beds, and will flower year after year.

Bulbs are most often bought in bags when they're dormant, in late summer and early autumn. However, they're also available as flowering

shapes and sizes. A wide range is available, in the form of 'plug' plants, young plants in multi-cell packs and as larger, in-bloom specimens (*see* page 45). You can also grow them from seed, which increases your options tenfold (*see* pages 46–8).

Biennials

Biennials are plants that grow from seed in their first year and then mature and flower in the next. They may live longer than two years, but are rarely as vigorous or floriferous in subsequent years and are usually

best dug up and discarded. Because they have already had a whole growing season, they often flower quite early in their second year, making them useful for colour in spring and early summer. Two common biennials – wallflowers (*Erysimum*) and double daisies (*Bellis perennis*) – both come into flower from mid-spring, while foxgloves (*Digitalis*) are just a little later.

Biennials tend to be reasonably straightforward to grow from seed, but you need somewhere to look after the plants before they reach

Don't forget

Bulbs you buy at the flowering stage will have been raised under cover, so even if they're hardy varieties they ought to be hardened off (*see* page 47) for a few days before planting out in the garden.

potted plants in spring. If you're well organized, it's best to buy them unplanted because this gives you a wider choice and is considerably less expensive, although it is wonderful to have the option of buying them ready to flower to brighten up beds and pots early in the year.

Tender perennials

Plants such as begonias, busy lizzies (*Impatiens*) and pelargoniums are classic tender perennials. Like annuals, they make good summer bedding in borders and they're also ideal for pots and hanging baskets. Cannas, dahlias and the banana-like *Ensete* also belong to this group and are valuable for extending summer colour into autumn. They often make quite large plants, so give displays a feeling of permanence.

Some tender plants, most notably dahlias, are sold as clumps of fleshy roots in spring. Where this is the case, put the roots into pots to grow to a reasonable size before planting them into their flowering positions.

All tender perennials would happily live for years in warmer climates, but they're not capable of withstanding heavy frost. However, you can keep many of them alive

from year to year, usually by bringing them indoors over winter (*see* page 52). They can be raised from seed, but are more easily propagated by cuttings.

Hardy perennials, shrubs and dwarf trees

In the constant search for ever-more-interesting instant displays, especially in autumn and winter, gardeners have started to use hardy perennials, shrubs and miniature trees as bedding. Many shrubs and trees are appreciated purely for their foliage and include a wide range of brightly coloured conifers and heathers, but some, such as skimmias, also have flowers and fruit. Popular perennials

include Christmas rose (*Helleborus niger*), which flowers through winter, and heucheras, grown for their lovely foliage. These plants can live for years, but there is nothing to say they cannot make a short-term contribution to a pot or temporary garden display. Afterwards, they can be transplanted to a permanent position in the garden or discarded.

Perennials, shrubs and miniature trees are sold in a range of sizes in containers. They are likely to be slightly more expensive than traditional bedding plants, but the price is worth it when you consider that they will work hard through the autumn and winter and that you can keep them for longer if you wish.

Purple heucheras and silver shrubby helichrysum make interesting fillers in this formal garden, where terracotta pots overflowing with pelargoniums create bright focal points.

Don't forget

There are a few hardy perennials, such as pansies (*Viola*) that are treated as annuals and discarded after flowering, mainly because they produce fewer flowers in subsequent years.

Design principles

No matter how informal or relaxed it looks, a pleasing garden will have been carefully thought through before being planted up. Whether you're planning to introduce seasonal colour to flower beds, borders or containers, it's always very helpful to understand a few basic principles of garden design.

A successful planting scheme must be harmonious and work as a whole as well as providing plenty of interest (*see* Design tips, opposite). Start by thinking about the effect you'd like to achieve, taking into account the season, location and your colour preferences. Ask yourself if you want a bright, lively display that attracts attention, or something subtler that quietly enhances a dull corner. Do you want to fill the whole garden with colour, or just have one or two striking containers in key positions?

Formal schemes

The formal bedding schemes used in parks and other public places usually consist of a patterned 'carpet' of low-growing annuals punctuated with a series of taller tender perennial 'dot' plants in contrasting colours. This type of planting looks wonderful in the right setting, but it is a challenge to get right. It requires many plants of the same size, shape and vigour;

all need to flower at the same time and with the same abundance; and if any die you need replacements to fill the gaps. The display may last several weeks, but then you need to remove the whole lot and start again. In most domestic gardens a formal display is best restricted to specific situations, such as a centrally placed island bed, a front-garden flower bed or a raised bed.

Informal schemes

Generally, it is wiser to aim for a more informal scheme, either using only bedding or by combining bedding with permanent plants. The latter looks more natural and helps

Blue larkspur, red poppies, orange pot marigolds and white begonias are carefully grouped to eye-catching effect in this informal annual border.

to augment the display and lengthen the season of interest. With this approach it's better to have a more restricted colour palette, although you can still make it eye-catching with plenty of contrasts if you wish. Use plants in drifts and groups rather than individually, and make full use of taller and medium-sized plants as well as smaller ones.

When planning informal schemes for the garden, try to choose plants that flower at different times, so you don't get everything at once, like a firework display. There are two main reasons for this: your flower beds will have areas of leafy quiet (not-yet-in-flower) and lively colour (in-flower), which will make the display interesting but not overwhelming,

This modern, formal bedding display is built with layers of plants including silver helichrysums and purple salvias with tall canna lilies as a focal point.

Design tips

■ Keep plantings simple by limiting yourself to just a few colours (see pages 14–16); with so many plants to choose from it's all too tempting to pick one of each and end up with something that looks like a broken kaleidoscope.

■ Include a variety of sizes, shapes and textures for interest (see pages 18–19), but again keep it simple.

■ Place several groups of the same plant through a flower bed to create a visual echo; this will help to draw together, or unite, the other elements.

■ Don't forget about foliage – it will provide a useful foil to set off other plants and can be the main attraction (see page 20).

■ When selecting containers (see page 33), choose those of a similar shape or colour – this produces a more pleasing result than having a mixed bag and means you can be more adventurous with the plants you put in them.

■ Containers often look better grouped together, particularly smaller ones. Also, grouping them reduces moisture loss and therefore the need for watering.

■ When planting up containers, select a mixture of feature, spreading and trailing plants (see pages 40–1).

and it will give you a much longer period of enjoyment. As plants fade and die, you can replace them with others to flower later.

Focal points

Whether you have a formal or an informal display, you'll need to think about focal points. These are spots that attract your attention when you gaze into the garden. It is always useful to have at least one and sometimes several. Tall bedding varieties are very effective: cannas, dahlias and other leafy plants such as *Ensete* are good candidates, since their strong foliage forms make them look interesting even when they're not in flower. Alternatively, try annual climbers, such as sweet peas (*Lathyrus*) and morning glory (*Ipomoea*), on attractive frames.

Using colour

From early spring until the depths of winter, bedding plants can be relied upon to provide brilliant and abundant colour in almost any part of the garden. When selecting colours, you will be more assured of success if you follow a few rules, or at least bear them in mind.

The colour wheel

The colour wheel is a simple way of seeing and understanding how colours relate to each other. It can be invaluable in helping you start to decide what colours you want to use and which ones will go together well. You can use it to make subtle colour combinations as well as more vibrant, contrasting ones.

Harmonizing colours are next to each other on the wheel. Choosing these colours will produce elegant combinations that are generally gentle on the eye. Contrasting colours are opposite each other. Using them together results in a more lively and dramatic effect. There are no rights and wrongs in going for either of these, or even a combination of both, but it does help to know the likely outcome of your choice.

Within each colour there is a huge number of variations, with stronger, deeper tones and more pastel hues completing the spectrum. For instance, if you decide to go for blue, you'll need to consider a wide range of shades from powder blue to navy blue, with any number of different hues in between, including lilac, lavender, violet and royal blue (*see* opposite).

A colour wheel is a quick guide to the way colours work together. Colours that are adjacent on the wheel are harmonious, while opposite ones are contrasting.

Red

A very common colour among bedding plants, red is strong and rich. It isn't called a 'hot' colour for nothing. If you want an attention-grabbing display, use it on its own or combine it with acid yellow or bright orange. Add lime green for even more zest. If you prefer something less challenging, choose strong, velvety reds. These can produce elegant displays, especially when they're planted with similarly rich, classy colours, such as violet or deep blue. Grey-green or purple

Don't forget

Try to include a range of flower colours, not just your favourites. A garden full of, say, pink is much less interesting than one where the pink is combined with grey-green, blue or white.

Acid-yellow and lime-green euphorbias provide a sensational backdrop for the hot orange and red of these tulips: a marriage of contrast and harmony.

foliage adds sumptuous undertones. For something gentler, choose a softer tone of red, such as pink-red or purple-red, and add some powder blue or creamy yellow. When used like this, the red will bring a touch of warmth without being dominant or overwhelming.

Orange and yellow

The purest shades of orange and yellow can be quite brash and demanding. It is tempting to think of them as a bit vulgar but, like a naughty schoolboy, they can also make you smile. They are the colours of early-flowering plants, such as daffodils (*Narcissus*), primulas and wallflowers (*Erysimum*), and in the late winter and early spring these bright, simple shades are most welcome. Used in moderation at any time of the year, they bring a bright, sunny, warm feeling into the garden.

Many bedding plants are available in softer shades and tones of both orange and yellow, including peach, apricot and primrose or a powder yellow, all of which are usually easy to combine with a wide variety of other colours. Apricot goes very well with salmon pink, for example, while powder yellow tends to look good with purple or pale blue.

Pink

Pink is related to red but tends to have a wider spectrum of variations and can range from hot to cool. Creamy pink is a warm colour, for instance, while blue-pink is a cool one. The warm shades are easier to integrate into subtle plantings and look particularly lovely combined with pale yellows, grey-greens and

Purple-blue *Salvia farinacea* and bluish-pink cosmos create a restful, harmonious picture in the low light of this summer garden.

pastel blues. Somewhat surprisingly, the cooler shades are often more strident and are effective in bolder displays mixed with orange or yellow. Alternatively, they can be used as an eye-catching accent in subtler colour combinations.

Blue, purple and violet

Like red, blue has a strong, bold character, but while red is fiery and hot, blue is cool and restful.

In its darker shades, such as purple and violet, blue is always elegant, blending into the background when planted with similar dark colours or standing out among less refined, brighter companions. It brings a sense of order and moderation, making it very useful for combining with some of the more vivid shades found in bedding plants.

Paler blues look good with such a wide range of colours that they make great filler plants and are almost never out of place. Powder

blue will tone down a bright yellow or make a perfect partner with creamy yellow, while lavender and lilac mix particularly well with strong pinks as well as paler ones.

True blue flowers are very rare, and most plants we consider blue tend to be tinged with other colours.

Black

In plants, the really dark shades, from bronze to nearly black, are usually made of reds and browns, although some are very dark green or blue. If you hold a dark leaf to the sun, you can see this clearly. Those that are made from reds are warm and are particularly spectacular positioned where the sun can shine

Don't forget

In direct sun, blue flowers can have a pinkish hue, so for harmonious schemes combine them with pinks and mauves. Adding a contrasting shade, such as orange, will help accentuate the blue tones.

The rich purple undertones of *Alternanthera* 'Royal Tapestry' bring out the soft red-orange in *Gazania* 'Daybreak Bronze'.

In this unusual colour combination the white arabis creates a crisp, snow-like bed for the daffodils (*Narcissus* 'Jetfire').

through them. They go well with other warm colours, such as orange and red. Green- or blue-blacks are cool and add to the elegance of blue schemes or those that include deep reds, and they can be used to tone down orange and yellow.

Green and grey-green

Green is all around us in the garden, so we tend not to notice it as much as other colours. However, it plays an extremely important part in planting schemes and is well worth

considering in your plans. It works in two ways: it counterbalances other colours and it is a colour in its own right. To understand the first role, think of a floral display as a piece of music – the foliage is like the pauses, the places to draw breath and slow down. Interspersing foliage plants among flowering ones both highlights the colours around them and provides areas of calm.

As with other colours, green comes in a wide variety of different shades. Grey-green is soft and subtle and is a lovely foil for pink or creamy yellow, while stronger lime greens can create sharp contrasts – with red or blue, for example. Dark green goes well with rich red and blue and bright green looks good with orange or yellow.

White

There are many different whites, ranging from a cool ice-white to warm creamy white. White flowers look wonderful in front of dark

foliage and can bring light into shady areas. Best used *en masse* – otherwise they can look bitty – they form a great backdrop and often have the effect of accentuating other colours, making displays crisper and more eye-catching. Yellow or orange and white are zingy combinations, while red or blue and white have a cool, clean look, softened by the addition of pink.

If you're feeling brave, you could devote whole areas of the garden, especially shady ones, to white. The results can be stunning, but keep the different shades of white to a minimum and have both large and small flowers, along with silver- or grey-green foliage, to provide additional interest.

Colour mixes and bicolours

Many bedding plants come in colour mixes. These combinations always look good together, but they can be difficult to combine with other flowers. One of the easiest solutions is to pick one colour from the mixture and choose partners for this. For example, in a mix that contains pinks, white and reds, choose colours to go with the pinks, such as creamy whites, pale yellows or soft blues.

Bicolours have two or more distinct colours in each bloom (*see* page 21). It is easiest to select just one of these to use in your colour combinations.

Don't forget

Pale colours, such as white, light yellow and pink, show up very well at dusk. The foliage fades into the dark and the flowers appear to float above the ground, adding an extra dimension to your garden.

Although bedding plants are chosen primarily for their decorative contribution, some also have a lovely fragrance, which makes them doubly valuable. It is always worth putting a few of these close to seating areas, in pots or hanging baskets beside the front door, or anywhere that you can appreciate their perfume.

Early perfume

For very early scent there's little to beat daffodils (*Narcissus*) and primulas. The big, blowsy daffodils have a very delicate fragrance that is evocative of spring, but it is the smaller-flowered ones that are often outstanding. These include 'Avalanche', 'Soleil d'Or', 'Grand Soleil d'Or', 'Pixie's Sister', 'Silver Chimes' and many more.

Among primulas it is those with yellow flowers that are the most strongly scented. The fragrance is especially noticeable if you put the plants in a warm, sheltered position.

Blooming just a little later, wallflowers (*Erysimum*) are amazingly generous in both flower and fragrance. Even if you don't want a bedful, just grow one or two in prime positions and breathe in deeply as you pass by.

Summer scents

The most obvious plants to grow for summer scent are the sweet peas (*Lathyrus*). There are many varieties and some are more fragrant than others, so check you're getting fragrant ones before you buy – the label should make this clear.

The lovely, deep violet-blue cherry pie (*Heliotropium arborescens* 'Marine')

Fragrance comes in many flower colours, shapes and sizes.

① *Nicotiana sylvestris*.
② *Narcissus* 'Soleil d'Or'.
③ *Matthiola longipetala* subsp. *bicornis*.
④ *Lathyrus odoratus*.

has the most gorgeous, fruity fragrance. Many of the nemesias are perfumed, but particularly look out for those with a hint in the name, such as Aromatica series, 'Fragrant Lady' and 'Vanilla Scent'. Some pelargoniums have scented foliage (*see* page 82).

Perfume at night

A few annuals emit their perfume at night to attract pollinating moths.

More fragrant flowers

Hyacinthus orientalis
Isotoma axillaris
Lobularia maritima
Matthiola incana
Petunia (particularly Tumbelina series)
Tulipa (some)
Viola Friolina series

These scented plants often have flowers that are closed in the daytime, which means you need to be careful how you position them: the last thing you want is a row of drooping blooms in full view during the day. However, you do want them easily accessible at night so you can drink in that wonderful fragrance. Night-scented plants include the tobacco plant *Nicotiana sylvestris*, which closes its flowers in full sun; night-scented stock (*Matthiola longipetala* subsp. *bicornis*), with flowers that look dead during the day but are perfumed at night; and night phlox (*Zaluzianskya capensis*), which opens at dusk.

Texture and form

The plants that are used to provide instant colour in gardens are usually very eye-catching, with abundant, showy flowers. For the majority, this is their main attraction, but to use them successfully in combination with other plants we ought to look beyond their colour. Whether we're conscious of it or not, flowers also make a contribution through their texture and form, and there are many bedding plants that are grown particularly for their interesting foliage or overall shape.

Texture

There are two aspects to texture: visual and tactile. Visual is probably more commonly thought of when it comes to plants, but you might be surprised to know how many people enjoy fondling, stroking and even squeezing flowers, leaves and stems, especially in gardens that belong to someone else! All this means that texture is important to us; we enjoy it and we benefit from its presence.

Small flowers and leaves look highly textured and tend to create a lively, busy effect. This is mainly due to the greater play of light and shade that occurs between them and the space around them – seen *en masse*, their effect is a bit like turning up the contrast on the television. By comparison, large flowers and big leaves, especially smooth or shiny ones, are calmer and gentler on the eye. To get the best out of both ends of the scale, you can intersperse small leaves and flowers with large ones. In traditional bedding schemes, this is where the dot plants often come in: where tulips are the 'dots', for example, forget-me-nots might provide the enlivening contrast. For less formal arrangements, you simply need to include a little of each to vary the mood and produce something that is appealing to look

In this thoughtful combination of texture and colour, fluffy *Ageratum* 'Blue Horizon' mingles with *Rudbeckia deamii* and a variegated bamboo.

Plants to feel

There are plenty of bedding plants that are tempting to touch. Here are a few highlights for the tactile gardener:

Antirrhinum – everyone knows what to do with the flowers of snapdragons!

Artemisia 'Powis Castle' – soft, feathery, aromatic leaves

Canna – smooth, shiny leaves and tissue-soft flowers

Celosia – dense, solid, cockscomb- or plume-like flowerheads

Cosmos bipinnatus – feathery leaves and beautifully pleated petals

Eschscholzia californica – feathery, aromatic foliage and silky, smooth petals

Helianthus annuus – big, rough-textured leaves and fascinating seedheads

Pelargonium – many varieties have softly furry, fragrant leaves

Pennisetum setaceum 'Rubrum' – softly strokable flowerheads

Petunia – velvety flowers

Salvia guaranitica 'Black and Blue' – surprisingly hard, rough leaves

Stipa tenuissima – long, soft, grassy leaves

The lovely yellow Lily-flowered tulip 'West Point' acts as an informal dot plant here, surrounded by a carpet of forget-me-nots.

at. For instances, when cannas are planted with taller salvias, such as *Salvia guaranitica* 'Black and Blue', the large, smooth canna leaves make a perfect counterpoint to the delicate spikes of the salvia flowers. On a smaller scale, the silvery, heart-shaped foliage of cyclamen looks positively graceful among the tough little leaves of heathers and heaths (*Calluna* and *Erica*).

Successful use of texture doesn't all have to be about extremes of size. You can achieve interesting effects by combining foliage and flowers of similar sizes but with very different shapes. Think spiky with smooth, such as ornamental grasses with busy lizzies (*Impatiens*), or airy with solid, such as verbena with petunias. Once you start to think about it, you can see texture everywhere.

Form

To a certain extent, texture and form go hand in hand – a large-leaved plant often has a tall, elegant form, while a small one is more likely to be rounded and compact. However, it is useful to think of them separately, because it can help you to decide where to place them in the garden.

For many years, it has been the fashion to breed bedding plants for more flowers and also to be small, even dwarf, to fit in pots, hanging baskets and narrow borders. They are also bred to be self-supporting, so have a tendency to be rather stiff and upright in form. All of these

The red and pink flowers (*Hemerocallis*, *Phlox*, *Dianthus* and *Lobelia*) might catch your eye first in this mixed planting, but the form and texture of the foliage plants (*Alchemilla*, *Euphorbia* and *Helichrysum*) come a very close second.

features are ideal when it comes to ease of maintenance, but a flower bed full of small, stiff, starchy plants is going to look – well ... stiff and starchy, and rather formal. If you're after something less regimented, the best way to avoid this effect is to choose a variety of plant shapes and sizes to break up the solidity of the display. Pick tall-stemmed, airy plants as well as short, neat ones with flowers that hug the stems, hiding all the foliage. Also, include trailing varieties and annual climbers in your display to provide a sense of informality.

Silver-leaved helichrysum softens the pink petunia flowers in this romantic colour mix, and the spikes and rounded shapes contrast beautifully.

Design palette

These lists should help you decide on planting schemes for beds and containers. Remember, within each colour there are many variations. Argyranthemums, calibrachoas, petunias, primulas, pansies and violas aren't listed as they're available in almost every colour. (For seasonal combinations, *see* pages 24–43.)

Leaf colour

BLUISH FOLIAGE
Chamaecyparis lawsoniana 'Ellwoodii'
Dianthus (many)
Festuca glauca 'Blaufuchs'
Festuca glauca 'Elijah Blue' (right)
Festuca glauca 'Intense Blue'
Juniperus communis 'Compressa'
Juniperus squamata 'Blue Star'
Lotus berthelotii
Picea pungens 'Globosa'

LIME-GREEN FOLIAGE
Bacopa 'Lime Delight'
Bacopa 'Scopia Golden Leaves'
Cupressus macrocarpa 'Goldcrest' (right)
Fuchsia magellanica 'Gold Mountain'
Helichrysum petiolare 'Limelight'
Heuchera 'Key Lime Pie'
Heuchera 'Lime Marmalade'
Ipomoea 'Marguerite'
Solenostemon 'Versa Lime'

WHITE-VARIEGATED FOLIAGE
Cyclamen persicum 'Winter Ice'
Euonymus fortunei 'Emerald Gaiety'
Euonymus japonicus 'Pierrolino'
Felicia amelloides 'Variegata'
Hedera helix 'Eva'
Heuchera 'Cinnabar Silver'
Heuchera 'Geisha's Fan'
Pelargonium 'L'Elégante' (right)
Plectranthus coleoides 'Variegata'

GOLD FOLIAGE
Artemisia 'Oriental Limelight'
Erica vulgaris 'Crimson Glory'
Euonymus fortunei 'Emerald 'n' Gold' (right)
Heuchera 'Amber Waves'
Heuchera 'Tara'
Impatiens 'Masquerade'
Salvia officinalis 'Icterina'
Thuja occidentalis Rheingold

ALMOST BLACK FOLIAGE
Aeonium arboreum 'Zwartkop' (right)
Ajuga 'Braunherz'
Alternanthera 'Purple Knight'
Antirrhinum 'Bronze Dragon'
Begonia 'Nonstop Mocca'
Dahlia 'Bishop of Llandaff'
Ophiopogon planiscapus 'Nigrescens'
Pennisetum glaucum 'Purple Majesty'
Solenostemon 'Dark Chocolate'

SILVER FOLIAGE
Artemisia 'Powis Castle'
Dichondra 'Silver Falls' (right)
Helichrysum italicum 'Korma'
Helichrysum 'Silver Mist'
Plectranthus 'Silver Crest'
Santolina chamaecyparissus
Senecio cineraria 'Cirrus'
Senecio cineraria 'Silver Dust'
Tanacetum argenteum

RED-VARIEGATED FOLIAGE
Ajuga 'Burgundy Glow'
Canna 'Phasion'
Coprosma 'Pacific Sunset'
Ensete ventricosum 'Maurelii'
Heuchera 'Miracle'
Pelargonium 'Blazonry'
Pelargonium 'Vancouver Centennial' (right)
Solenostemon 'Saturn'

PURPLE OR BRONZE FOLIAGE
Aeonium arboreum 'Atropurpureum'
Alternanthera 'Royal Tapestry'
Antirrhinum 'Black Prince'
Canna 'King Humbert'
Dahlia 'David Howard'
Heuchera 'Obsidian'
Heuchera 'Plum Pudding' (right)
Impatiens New Guinea hybrids (many)
Pennisetum setaceum 'Fireworks'

Flower colour

WHITE FLOWERS

Ageratum 'Timeless'
Anemone blanda 'White Splendour'
Antirrhinum 'Royal Bride'
Bacopa 'Snowflake' (right)
Cosmos bipinnatus 'Purity'
Crocus 'Snow Bunting'
Dahlia 'Twyning's After Eight'
Fuchsia 'Hawkshead'
Gypsophila elegans 'Covent Garden'
Impatiens 'Accent White'
Lobularia maritima 'Clear Crystal White'

BLUE FLOWERS

Ageratum (many)
Anemone blanda 'Blue Shades' (right)
Centaurea cyanus 'Blue Diadem'
Heliotropium 'Marine'
Hyacinthus 'Delft Blue'
Ipomoea 'Heavenly Blue'
Iris reticulata 'Harmony'
Isotoma axillaris
Lobelia 'Crystal Palace'
Nemesia 'Royal Blue'
Salvia patens

PINK FLOWERS

Ageratum 'Tutti Booties'
Antirrhinum 'Eternal'
Clarkia elegans 'Apple Blossom'
Cyclamen persicum
Dahlia 'Roxy'
Dianthus chinensis 'Baby Doll'
Diascia 'Wink Pink'
Nemesia 'Amelie'
Osteospermum 'Serenity Pink' (right)
Pelargonium 'Maverick Appleblossom'
Tulipa 'Angélique'

PURPLE, VIOLET & BLACK FLOWERS

Angelonia 'Serena Purple'
Calibrachoa 'Cabaret Lavender'
Centaurea cyanus 'Black Ball' (right)
Dahlia 'Black Narcissus'
Fritillaria meleagris
Lophospermum erubescens 'Burgundy Falls'
Rhodochiton atrosanguineus
Salvia guaranitica 'Black and Blue'
Tropaeolum 'Black Velvet'
Verbena 'Quartz Purple'

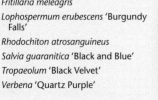

RED FLOWERS

Ageratum 'Red Sea'
Ageratum 'Timeless'
Amaranthus caudatus
Antirrhinum 'Black Prince'
Begonia 'Million Kisses Devotion'
Centaurea cyanus 'Red Boy'
Cyclamen 'Miracle Scarlet'
Dahlia 'Arabian Night' (right)
Pelargonium 'Tom Cat'
Salvia coccinea 'Lady in Red'
Tulipa 'Apeldoorn'

YELLOW FLOWERS

Antirrhinum 'Peaches and Cream'
Begonia 'Sherbet Bon Bon'
Bidens (most)
Centaurea moschata 'Dairy Maid'
Dahlia 'Moonfire' (right)
Euryops pectinatus
Narcissus (many)
Rudbeckia 'Prairie Sun'
Sanvitalia procumbens
Tagetes (most)
Tropaeolum 'Peach Melba'

ORANGE FLOWERS

Antirrhinum 'Orange Glow'
Begonia 'Apricot Shades'
Calendula officinalis
Dahlia 'So Dainty'
Diascia 'Wink Orange' (right)
Erysimum 'Apricot Twist'
Eschscholzia californica
Pelargonium 'Angeleyes Orange'
Tagetes (most)
Tropaeolum 'Double Delight Apricot'
Tulipa 'Prinses Irene'

BICOLOURED FLOWERS

Dahlia 'Dahlietta Surprise Becky'
Dianthus 'Sunflor Bianca'
Fuchsia (most)
Gaillardia pulchella 'Arizona Sun'
Gazania 'Tiger Stripes' (right)
Mimulus 'Magical Blotched Mixed'
Nemesia 'KLM'
Pelargonium 'Happy Face Mex'
Pericallis 'Senetti'
Petunia 'Frenzy Star Mixed'
Torenia 'Clown Mixed'

Plants for a purpose

With so many options available, choosing bedding plants can be quite a challenge. Use the lists in this section to help you find the right plant for the job, bearing in mind the particular conditions in your garden and the effect you want to achieve in your borders and containers. Refer, too, to the directory of Recommended Bedding Plants on pages 56–91.

Verbena Aztec series is a great performer, flowering all summer long. It has a wonderful trailing habit and is ideal for hanging baskets.

Best for shade

Ajuga reptans
Anemone blanda
Begonia semperflorens
Carex oshimensis 'Evergold'
Erica carnea
Euonymus fortunei
Fuchsia
Gaultheria mucronata
Gaultheria procumbens
Hedera helix
Helleborus niger
Heuchera
Impatiens
Leucothoe
Lobelia
Mimulus
Narcissus
Skimmia japonica 'Rubella'
Solenostemon
Torenia

Best for windy sites

Argyranthemum
Felicia
Gazania
Iberis umbellata
Limonium sinuatum
Lobularia maritima
Pelargonium
Sanvitalia procumbens
Senecio maritima
Tagetes
Tropaeolum
Zinnia

Best for tiny spaces

Ajuga reptans
Brassica
Calluna vulgaris
Cyclamen persicum
Erica carnea
Festuca glauca 'Intense Blue'
Iberis umbellata
Impatiens
Lobularia maritima
Nemesia
Nemophila
Ophiopogon planiscapus 'Nigrescens'
Oxalis triangularis
Primula
Sanvitalia procumbens

Best for hot spots

Alternanthera
Argyranthemum
Celosia
Cleome spinosa
Eschscholzia californica
Euryops pectinatus
Gaillardia
Gazania
Limonium sinuatum
Osteospermum
Pelargonium
Salpiglossis sinuata
Sanvitalia procumbens
Tithonia
Tropaeolum
Zinnia

Best edible ornamentals

Basil
Chillies
Chives
Lettuce
Parsley
Peppers
Runner beans
Strawberries
Swiss chard
Thyme

Best for large flowers

Abutilon
Anemone coronaria De Caen Group
Argyranthemum
Begonia tuberhybrida
Cosmos
Dahlia
Helianthus annuus
Hyacinthus
Ipomoea purpurea
Osteospermum
Pelargonium
Petunia
Ranunculus asiaticus
Rudbeckia
Tagetes 'French Vanilla'
Tagetes Taishan series
Tulipa

Best tall plants

Amaranthus caudatus
Canna (most)
Cleome spinosa
Cosmos bipinnatus
Consolida ajacis
Dahlia (many)
Ensete ventricosum 'Maurelii'
Helianthus annuus (many)
Lavatera trimestris 'Loveliness'
Nicotiana sylvestris
Ricinus communis
Rudbeckia (many)
Strobilanthes dyerianus

Best for a rounded habit

Anemone blanda
Argyranthemum
Begonia tuberhybrida
Calendula officinalis
Erysimum
Euryops pectinatus
Fuchsia (many)
Limnanthes
Osteospermum
Santolina chamaecyparissus
Schizanthus
Tagetes (some)
Torenia
Viola

Best for a trailing habit

Bacopa
Bidens ferulifolia
Calibrachoa
Dichondra
Hedera helix
Lobelia
Lophospermum
Petunia
Plectranthus coleoides
Rhodochiton atrosanguineus
Sanvitalia
Tropaeolum
Verbena
Viola Friolina series

Best low-growing plants

Ageratum
Begonia semperflorens
Bellis perennis
Calceolaria
Dianthus chinensis
Diascia (some)
Heuchera (all)
Impatiens (many)
Lobularia
Mimulus
Nemophila
Oxalis triangularis
Primula

Best for an upright habit

Ageratum (many)
Angelonia
Antirrhinum
Celosia
Clarkia
Cleome
Fritillaria
Gladiolus
Matthiola (some)
Molucella
Papaver somniferum
Phlox drummondii
Salvia
Tagetes (some)
Zantedeschia

Best easy-grow plants

Antirrhinum
Begonia semperflorens
Crocus
Eschscholzia californica
Iberis umbellata
Impatiens
Laurentia axillaris
Linaria 'Northern Lights'
Lobularia maritima
Mimulus
Nicotiana dwarf types
Nigella damascena

Best for soft effects

Artemisia 'Powis Castle'
Bidens ferulifolia
Brachyscome
Cosmos bipinnatus
Diascia
Eschscholzia
Euphorbia 'Diamond Frost'
Felicia
Gypsophila elegans
Isotoma axillaris
Lagurus ovatus
Myosotis sylvatica
Nemesia
Nigella
Papaver rhoeas
Senecio cineraria 'Silver Dust'

Prefer neutral to acid soil

Begonia
Calceolaria
Calluna
Clarkia
Erica
Nemesia

Prefer alkaline soil

Amaranthus
Centaurea
Dianthus
Erysimum
Iberis umbellata
Matthiola
Pelargonium

Tolerate low-fertility soil

Amaranthus caudatus
Anchusa capensis
Calendula officinalis
Erica
Eschscholzia californica
Gaillardia
Limonium sinuatum
Lobularia maritima

Colour for all seasons

The greatest advantage of bedding plants is that they can provide you with instant colour in your garden every month of the year. For best results you need to think of these plants as being similar to flowers in the house: you bring them in, arrange them carefully, enjoy them while they're in their prime and then put them on the compost heap. Meanwhile, you're working on the next display to take their place. This sort of attitude goes against the grain for many gardeners – we're used to making things last and waiting for our rewards – but it can be great fun, and creative too.

Planning your schemes

It's perfectly possible to go to the garden centre, buy a trolley-load of plants and have a garden full of colour later the same day. However, it's important to plan ahead and know more or less what you want to buy before you get there. If you don't, the choice can be overwhelming and you may well make costly mistakes, selecting plants that don't suit the site or won't work with neighbouring plants. Planning now will save you money, time and effort and will bring you much more satisfying results.

If you plan ahead and sow annuals direct in spring (*see* page 48), you can have many weeks of bright colour throughout the summer.

Considering colour

Try to think about spring colour in autumn and summer colour in spring. First, appraise your garden and decide exactly what you're hoping to achieve. The very fact that you're thinking about adding colour means you already know you have areas that could do with a facelift at certain times of the year. Narrow these down. When and where would you like more colour or more to look at? And how much colour do you want: would you like to fill a whole flower bed with summer flowers or just brighten up dull areas within existing borders? Perhaps you have seating areas that could do with a

few colourful pots, or shady corners calling out for some floral interest. Consider your style and whether you like formal, naturalistic, modern or traditional effects. Think about the sorts of colours you like and which of them work well together (*see* pages 14–16 and 21).

It's easy to get carried away, so remember to consider the overall ambience of your garden and work on ways to jazz up particular areas without disturbing the tranquillity elsewhere. Perhaps focus on livening up one flower bed and leave others as they are. Also, think about what will happen when those flowers fade and you're looking for colour for another few months.

Choosing plants

As well as selecting plants for their flowers, remember to include an interesting mixture of plant textures and forms (*see* pages 18–19). Foliage is important too, as it sets off flowers beautifully, can be an attraction in its own right and extends the season of interest (*see* page 20).

The pages that follow provide information about the sorts of plants that look good through the different seasons, and the plants described in the directory (*see* pages 56–91) will give you more ideas, too. Once you have done your research, set out your ideas – make a few notes, jot down the names of suitable plants and draw a sketch or two.

Don't forget

There's plenty of scope for grand schemes in late spring, summer and early autumn, but you'll need to be content with more moderate displays for late autumn and winter.

The vast choice of colours, sizes and shapes available in modern bedding plants has given garden designers the equivalent of a three-dimensional painter's palette to play with. In addition, many bedding plants quickly reach flowering size and bloom for weeks on end, making them excellent for experimentation. Contemporary designs range from fairly formal layouts with a modern twist to adventurous naturalistic planting. The results are often stunning.

Naturalistic drifts

Probably the most impressive modern use of annuals is to plant or sow them in great swathes or drifts, mimicking how they might appear in nature (*see* 2, right). For the best results, choose varieties that are close to their wild ancestors in habit, such as poppies (*Papaver*), cornflowers (*Centaurea cyanus*), California poppies (*Eschscholzia californica*) and love-in-a-mist (*Nigella damascena*). Relatively lax, informal forms are key to success; you'll get a parade-ground feel if you use upright plants bred to be short and compact. Limiting the selection to just one or two varieties increases the natural feel, too. A good trick is to have a single major colour theme with just a smattering of a minor colour running through it. Or you could focus on contrasting plant forms or leaf textures.

Classy blocks and rows

A new take on bedding schemes is the use of more refined colour combinations and blocks of colour rather than the traditional schemes of patterned

Bedding plants fit easily into many different styles of gardening.
① Rows of swan river daisy (*Brachyscome*) and pot marigolds (not yet in flower).
② Drifts of California poppies (*Eschscholzia californica*) and purple-blue *Phacelia tanacetifolia*.
③ Pale yellow *Dahlia* 'Clair de Lune' mingles with variegated miscanthus.

'carpets' interspersed with contrasting dot plants. The result can be bolder than traditional layouts, but by the same token less challenging. Rather than shouting 'Look at me!' the plants say, 'I'm here to be appreciated.'

Among the best choices for block planting are cannas, with their paddle-shaped leaves and upright habit; also, bright-red-flowered salvias make a great partnership with orange

and red gaillardias. In the right setting, rows of smaller plants (*see* 1, above) look as good as blocks and produce a subtle formality.

Mingling with other plants

Some of the most elegant schemes come from interweaving bedding plants with more permanent planting, particularly grasses and other plants with gentle textures that can absorb the stronger shapes of the bedding. The bold flowers of dahlias look wonderful softened by the indistinct shapes of ornamental grasses, for example (*see* 3, above), while feathery fern foliage is perfect for moderating the stiff outlines of plants such as begonias or busy lizzies (*Impatiens*).

Spring borders

After a long, drab winter we're all in need of something to brighten up our lives, and if you're short of colour in your garden, spring is probably the time you'll notice it the most. Fortunately, since there is very little competition from many of the more permanent plants in the garden – they are still leafless or just emerging from the soil – it doesn't take much in the way of additions to make an impact.

Early spring

Primulas, double daisies (*Bellis perennis*), pansies (*Viola*), anemones, hyacinths (*Hyacinthus*) and lots of other bulbs, including the lovely dwarf bulbous Reticulata Group irises, are the best bet for drops of colour early in the year. Small pots are available in spring as they come into flower; just plunge these into the ground. If you're well organized, plant bulbs *en masse* in borders in autumn. This will give you more colour for your money and will make it easier to have a widespread, natural-looking display. Concentrate on areas close to the house.

For hot, bright displays choose pansies and primulas, which are available in a range of very strong colours, including reds, purples and yellows. They look lovely planted in large groups in borders or in sinuous 'ribbons' alongside paths and steps. For something more restrained, use paler flowers, such as snowdrops (*Galanthus*) with crocuses, or white daffodils (*Narcissus*) with anemones and soft-pink double daisies.

A little bit later

As the days lengthen and the sun gets warmer, our craving for colour tends to increase. In late spring, there are few plants that are more satisfying than a blanket of bright tulips or, particularly if you want scent, wallflowers (*Erisymum*). In both formal and informal schemes, tulips are traditionally underplanted with forget-me-nots (*Myosotis*) or pansies, since these short plants disguise the long stems of the tulips and provide an excellent foil too. If you're looking for bold, sunny combinations, choose cerise and violet or bright yellow and red; for a cooler and more refined effect, use softer pinks, blues and pale yellows.

Don't overlook the possiblities of evergreen foliage. There are several euonymus, including 'Emerald 'n' Gold' with yellow-variegated leaves, that will provide welcome colour and look good with a range of spring flowers including the tulips and forget-me-nots. (For spring container ideas, *see* pages 34–5.)

Don't forget

If you have only an hour to spare in the autumn, spend it choosing and planting tulip bulbs. They will give you almost any colour combination under the sun and repay your hour tenfold in the spring.

A hot place to sit on a spring day: wallflower *Erysimum* 'Fire King' flanks red tulips, yellow irises and acid-green euphorbias in this vibrant display.

Summer borders

As spring gives way to summer, the garden burgeons with unfurling leaves and opening flowers and there is the promise of more to come. At this time of year, bedding has two main roles: it contributes to the overall appearance of the garden and adds colour at a time when other flowers are lacking. Even if you have a good selection of permanent plants, you can use bedding for additional colour, structure or focal points.

Informal displays

One of the simplest ways to use bedding is in informal schemes. Make these up using a selection of plants you like, experimenting with different colours and plant shapes. To begin with, it's easier to combine them with the permanent plants already in your borders, but once you know the plants and how they perform in your garden, you can devote whole beds to them. When successful these can be stunning,

but it does take a bit of practice to get it right. Although you can sow seeds for these displays, you might prefer to use pot-grown plants, as the results are more immediate.

Cool schemes

Cool colours include whites, purples, blues and blue-pinks, and a lovely and very straightforward cool combination is blue cornflowers (*Centaurea cyanus*) and pink cosmos. Not only do the flowers look good together, but the feathery, pale green leaves of the cosmos are also perfect with the stiffer but equally attractive grey-green leaves of the cornflower. For a greater contrast, pick *Salvia farinacea* instead of cornflowers. This is upright with spikes of flowers that create a stronger structural element.

If you want a lower-growing plant for the front of the bed, use *Salvia viridis*, with its vivid, leaf-like bracts in a range of violets, pinks and white. It looks particularly effective with pink diascias, which are more delicate, or yellow marigolds

This semi-formal scheme consists of blue ageratums, pale pink cosmos and dark-purple-leaved cannas in loose rows around a gently curving lawn.

Often the simplest ideas are the best. Here the purple-leaved fountain grass *Pennisetum setaceum* 'Atropurpureum' is combined with white cosmos.

Hot, bright colours are mixed in this exuberant display: lipstick-pink and magenta zinnias, yellow and orange marigolds and pink cosmos.

(*Tagetes*), which will bring a little brightness to the mix. The more relaxed habit of the single-flowered varieties is best for informal schemes. Pale yellow shows up in the twilight, extending your enjoyment of the garden into the evening.

More combinations

COOL SCHEMES

Consolida ajacis 'Moody Blues' & *Gypsophila elegans* 'Covent Garden'

Lavatera trimestris 'Mont Blanc' & *Penstemon* 'Blackbird'

Papaver rhoeas 'Angel's Choir' & *Centaurea cyanus* 'Black Ball'

Salvia viridis & *Nigella damascena*

WARM SCHEMES

Antirrhinum 'Liberty' & *Lagurus ovatus*

Dahlia 'Art Deco' & *Oxalis triangularis*

Helianthus annuus 'Pastiche' & *Cleome spinosa* 'Colour Fountain'

HOT SCHEMES

Canna 'Striata' & *Rudbeckia* 'Prairie Sun'

Eschscholzia californica 'Thai Silk' & *Linaria maroccana* 'Northern Lights'

Pennisetum glaucum 'Purple Majesty' & *Tithonia rotundifolia* 'Torch'

Tagetes Bonanza series & *Solenostemon* 'Versa Lime'

Warm schemes

Warm colours include creamy whites, peachy yellows, pale oranges and creamy or red-pinks. They are subtle and gentle but can still be striking. Bicoloured flowers in these shades often have a softer effect than single colours. For example, dahlias such as 'Moonfire' (creamy-yellow flowers with orange centres) or 'Bishop of Oxford' (orange flowers with darker centres) have a warm glow that is perfectly offset by their dark bronze foliage. In combination with flowers that pick out one or the other of these shades they look very alluring. Snapdragons (*Antirrhinum*) in yellow, orange or peach work well, their upright shape counterbalancing the bulkier dahlias. Other spiky plants, such as grasses or gladiolus, are good too.

Hot schemes

Hot beds are deservedly popular and can look tremendous. Made up from plants at the red, orange and yellow end of the spectrum, they usually contain red dahlias, such as 'Bishop of Llandaff', as well as other richly coloured tender perennials, like cannas and castor oil plant (*Ricinus*). The elegant scarlet spikes of *Salvia* 'Lady in Red' and the thick crimson-purple tassels of love-lies-bleeding (*Amaranthus caudatus*) look good in this sort of scheme, too.

The key is to balance the reds with other colours. You can go for shades that are equally warm, such as yellow rudbeckias and orange gaillardias, or in complete contrast, try something cooler: dark blue *Salvia guaranitica* 'Black and Blue' or love-in-a mist (*Nigella damascena*) are suitable. Both are shortish with comparatively small flowers, so need to be planted in quantity.

Formal displays

Annuals often fill the spaces in knot gardens, where monochromatic schemes and clipped box hedges are used to create symmetrical patterns. Inside this neat frame, it takes a bit of courage to use just one colour,

A neat, evergreen hedge of clipped box provides a formal frame for a billowing combination of pink diascias and purple-blue heliotrope.

but it can be extremely striking, particularly if it is in a clearly defined area, such as beside a path or in a courtyard. White is popular, but red or blue would be equally effective, and pink can be easier on the eye. The downside of monochromatic schemes is that they can be hard to take day in, day out; just a tiny addition of a different shade could add interest and variety.

An alternative is to choose plants for their foliage effect. As well as tall cannas and castor oil plants, good foliage plants include the shorter, silvery *Senecio cineraria* 'Cirrus' or 'Silver Dust', a number of silver and gold helichrysums and the black-leaved, grass-like, ground-hugging *Ophiopogon planiscapus* 'Nigrescens'. A combination of these in a formal garden setting would look stunning. (For more on summer foliage plants and grasses, *see* pages 79–83.)

Filling the gaps

Sometimes, despite all your best efforts, gaps are bound to appear in your borders: flowers may be late opening or fade too soon, or new plants may fail to fill their allotted space. There is also the necessary rejuvenating of borders, after which it will take a couple of years for the inmates to grow together again and reach their full potential. On all of these occasions, bedding plants have an invaluable part to play.

Choose temporary plants with the same care that you'd pick permanent ones. In most cases, it's best to go for tallish varieties or those with a lax, spreading habit. These will sit more comfortably with the spreading mounds of, say, hardy geraniums, hellebores and oriental poppies (*Papaver orientale*), and complement the more defined forms of daylilies (*Hemerocallis*), eryngiums and astilbes. Generally, try to use single colours or mixtures in graduated, rather than contrasting, shades.

Good choices for planting at the front of a border include verbenas and diascias, which have soft forms, but you could equally well use Semperflorens-type begonias. Very short with succulent foliage and small flowers, these are available in subtle hues, such as white or pale pink with bronze foliage, and they're very easy to grow. Sweet alyssum (*Lobularia maritima*) is also good at the front of beds where its scent can be appreciated.

Taller plants for mingling and interweaving within borders include *Ageratum* 'Blue Horizon', which reaches 45cm (18in) high, and field poppies (*Papaver rhoeas*), which can grow as tall as 90cm (3ft). Phlox (*Phlox drummondii*) and *Clarkia* are available in taller forms too. Don't overlook the pale yellow or dark red sunflowers (*Helianthus annuus*), or the many annual salvias, in a range of blue, purple and red shades.

(For summer container ideas, *see* pages 36–9.)

Combining edible plants and flowers

Bright orange marigolds and the dense, mound-like leaves of English parsley look as if they were made for each other.

In summer, bedding plants make a big difference in the vegetable patch, where they provide additional interest and a splash of colour among the varied foliage and often more reserved flowers of the vegetables and herbs. If you have a formal veg garden with lots of neat lines, slip in a row of low-growing marigolds (*Calendula* or *Tagetes*), or go for bolder, taller displays of flowers for cutting, such as stocks (*Matthiola*), lavatera and cornflowers (*Centaurea cyanus*). With a little care, you can create some lovely colour combinations, such as red-toned beetroot leaves with violet-flowered stocks or pink lavatera, and bright green lettuce with rich-red nasturtiums (*Tropaeolum*). Everlasting flowers (*see* page 78) look wonderful in the veg garden too, particularly the upright statice (*Limonium*). (For edible ornamentals, *see* page 22.)

Climbing annuals and tender perennials

Annuals and tender perennials that climb and scramble are among the most valuable contributors to the summer garden. The speed at which they grow is one of their greatest attributes, and their slight and temporary nature means that they can be easily accommodated in almost any position, for a short while. They can screen, disguise and decorate unattractive areas or create a focal point. (*See also* pages 84–5.)

Screening and disguising

If given plenty of sun and water, nasturtiums (*Tropaeolum majus*) will scramble anywhere and can grow quite thickly. They're ideal for covering a fence or wall. They naturally scramble and trail, so need a bit of help to climb.

Tropaeolum peregrinum is more likely to grow upwards without help and has lovely yellow flowers. Spanish flag (*Ipomoea lobata*) is a vigorous tender perennial with lashings of lobed leaves and spikes of cream, yellow and orange flowers – ideal for drawing your eye away from an unprepossessing vista.

Decorating

The lovely bicoloured mauve bells of *Rhodochiton atrosanguineus* are often seen draped on decorative trellis and obelisks. A delicate plant, too fine for heavy-duty screening work, this tender perennial has heart-shaped leaves and eye-catching flowers. Suitable for similar situations but more robust, the perennial lofos (*Lophospermum*) is available in purple and creamy-white forms. It is also excellent when allowed

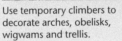

Use temporary climbers to decorate arches, obelisks, wigwams and trellis.
① *Ipomoea lobata*.
② *Tropaeolum* 'Alaska'.
③ *Ipomoea* 'Heavenly Blue' growing with non-climbing *Arctotis* × *hybrida* 'Flame'.
④ *Cobaea scandens*.

to trail from hanging baskets and down walls and fences.

Much brighter, the jewel-like flowers of another perennial, Chilean glory flower (*Eccremocarpus scaber*), look their best when this stiff-stemmed, rather untidy vine is allowed to scramble through another plant.

Cup-and-saucer vine (*Cobaea scandens*) is more elegant but very strong-growing. It is suitable for covering a large area, provided it is reasonably sheltered. It has attractive leaflets with twining tendrils and very solid-looking, large flowers that open white and age to blue-purple.

Focal points

For focal points, choose attractive climbing frames, such as metal or wooden obelisks, or make your own rustic ones from bamboo or hazel stakes. Sweet peas (*Lathyrus*) are the perfect plants for growing up these, but make sure you can get at them to pick the flowers. Morning glory (*Ipomoea*) is also lovely, especially 'Heavenly Blue'. Black-eyed susan (*Thunbergia alata*) is a dense climber that is brightly decorative and creates bold pyramids of orange or yellow. However, it has soft foliage that needs a reasonably sheltered spot.

Autumn and winter borders

As the days cool down and evenings begin to shorten, gardeners are very aware that all too soon flowers and leaves will disappear from flower beds. Nevertheless, there's still plenty of colour to be had in the garden if you know where to look.

Autumn schemes

Autumn is a very colourful time of the year, with berries and foliage brightening every corner. To boost the colour in your borders, have a look for a few late-flowering dahlias, which you might still be able to get at garden centres and will give you a few more weeks of bloom. Along with bedding chrysanthemums, they come in a range of bold colours that can make your display even brighter than in summer.

If you prefer something more naturalistic, *Cyclamen persicum* varieties, such as 'Miracle', are sold in bargain-priced packs at this time of year; they might be small, but they're extremely colourful and long-lasting.

It's well worth investing in heaths and heathers, too. These tough plants are not really very fashionable right now, which is a shame because they have attractive foliage ranging from lime green to rich gold and flowers from dark pink to white; *Erica carnea* produces these from

Early autumn is still full of promise. In this richly coloured, purple-and-pink-themed border, magenta dahlias and cerise gladioli jostle with soft-purple cleome.

winter into spring. Their traditional partners are conifers, but if you're after a low-level display, you could try them with cyclamen or with other evergreens including euonymus, heucheras and ivies.

Winter displays

There's no denying that winter can be drab, gloomy and dull. However, with a bit of ingenuity you can still have something to look at and enjoy.

In recent years, a huge selection of heucheras has become available and there are now more than anyone could grow in a single garden. Many retain their leaves all year round in sheltered spots, so choose a couple of the brighter-leaved ones: 'Crème Brûlée' is almost custard-coloured but also has bronzy tints, while the slightly more restrained 'Peach Flambé' turns from peach-pink to plum-purple in winter. For foliage contrasts, pick *Euonymus fortunei* 'Emerald Gaiety', which has small, white-variegated leaves that take on a pink tinge in winter, or choose a grass such as *Festuca glauca* 'Intense Blue' for this job. (For autumn and winter containers, *see* pages 42–3.)

Heucheras are extremely useful in the winter garden. Here, 'Obsidian' is a fine partner for the sedge *Carex oshimensis* 'Evergold' and a pink heath.

Instant colour for containers

Bedding plants are wonderful in the open garden, but there are some that simply excel in containers. Many of the modern varieties have been specifically bred or improved for pots, window boxes and hanging baskets. They tend to be small, or even dwarf, with more flowers than foliage, and being raised off the ground enables them to show off their generous flower displays to perfection. Many of these plants actually prefer the growing conditions offered by containers.

Choosing plants

Even if they're going to be together for only a short while, plants grown in the same pot need to like similar growing conditions, so make this a priority when planning your container schemes. If you're buying young plants to put into your pots, check the labels to find out the conditions they require; if growing your own (see box, below), check the seed packet. It's also important that the plants flower at the same time, so choose appropriately – a week or two either way won't make much difference, since flowering is hard to predict precisely anyway.

Selecting containers

Containers come in a huge range of sizes, shapes and materials and, within reason, you can pick anything that takes your fancy – from conventional containers such as pots, window boxes and hanging baskets to somewhat quirky, ad hoc options such as old food cans, tin baths, chimneys, old troughs or sinks and so on. Materials for pots include terracotta, stone, glazed earthenware, shiny steel and coloured fibreglass, and shapes can be square, round, tall or short – the variety is endless. Bear in mind that grouped plantings look much better if your pots match or are at least complementary. A row of similarly coloured pots will provide cohesion in even the most disparate planting.

Some hanging baskets are made of woven willow or other decorative materials, but plastic-covered wire baskets or just plastic ones are more widespread and really you don't want to see any part of them. This means that the aim is to fill the basket with plants to hide completely what is beneath (see page 50).

Practical considerations

Whatever style of container you choose, bear in mind that it must be fairly stable, needs at least one drainage hole and has to be suitable for outdoor use. For winter displays, choose thick, frost-proof pots.

Consider size, too. Larger plants need more space and potting compost than smaller ones and are more likely to suffer from drought in a small pot. By the same token, putting tiny plants in big containers is detrimental because they have smaller root systems, so are much more easily overwatered in a large pot; also, they'll lack visual impact.

Flowers and foliage plants are all good candidates for containers. The traditional pink pelargoniums and fuchsias are joined here by purple-leaved aeoniums and heucheras.

Growing your own

If you plan to grow your own plants from seed, start about six to eight weeks in advance and be prepared to pot up (transplant individual seedlings into bigger pots) at least once before your plants will be big enough to go into a container for display (see pages 46–7).

Don't forget

It is very difficult to remove large plants from their container if it has a rim that is narrower than the base.

Containers for spring

No matter where we live – whether in a city, town, village or the countryside – we can sense when spring is around the corner. This usually awakens an urge to get outside and enjoy the first signs of growth, yet it's often too cold or wet to spend much time outdoors. Containers are an incredibly useful way of bringing colour close to the house, with pots and window boxes filled with bulbs and other early-flowering plants.

Crocuses, such as *Crocus vernus*, come into their own planted in large groups in smallish containers.

Bright and cheery

There's nothing quite like yellow for brightening up a dingy corner or providing a cheery welcome by the front door, and this colour comes in abundance in spring.

The most obvious plants for a good dash of yellow are daffodils (*Narcissus*), and all can be grown in pots. The smaller varieties are most suitable and readily available in flower from garden centres, but even larger ones will give you a season of colour, after which they should be planted out. Daffs tend to have a stiff, upright habit, so soften them with other plants. *Cupressus macrocarpa* 'Goldcrest' is a good partner to give some structure as well as adding texture. This yellow-green conifer is commonly sold for pots, but must be considered only as a temporary resident, because it is fast-growing and could soon take over. Primulas are a good choice to fill around the base. You could go for a harmonizing yellow or have a contrast, such as blue or red. Add an evergreen trailing plant such as ivy (*Hedera*) or euonymus to swathe the pot and complete the picture.

Bright combinations look good in terracotta pots, which provide a warm undertone. Alternatively, containers with coloured glazes add to the colour display – blue, black or turquoise look good with yellow.

Subtle and elegant

If your preference is for something more refined, or unusual, choose the tiny early irises; *Iris* 'Harmony' is royal blue and 'J.S. Dijt' is red-purple. You'll find these, as well as others, in pots at the garden centre.

Accentuated by the yellow-green leaves of *Cornus controversa* 'Variegata', huge pots of *Tulipa* 'Purissima' look striking in this spring garden.

Don't forget

Large pots filled with one type of plant – for instance, blue hyacinths or yellow pansies – make a bold and attractive centrepiece.

Like daffodils, irises are stiff in habit, so complement this shape with the more spreading forms of small violas in a matching colour or with anemones, which have daisy-like flowers. Pick shallow, bowl-shaped containers, so as not to dwarf the plants, or choose pots with a simple decoration that will complement the flowers. For a classy, alpine-house look, use terracotta pans and cover the soil surface with fine grit.

Also ideal for bowls and pans, crocuses look good placed on walls or outdoor tables, where their markings can be best appreciated. Among the loveliest are those with contrasting stippling or sketchy stripes; *Crocus vernus* 'Pickwick' has rivulets of mauve both inside and out, while *Crocus* 'Ladykiller' is white with deep purple on the outside of the petals. Equally lovely are the creamy-yellow ones such as 'E.A. Bowles' and 'Cream Beauty'.

This is a stunning mixture of colours and flower form with *Tulipa* 'Abu Hassan' towering over bright primulas and forget-me-nots.

The pink, daisy-like flowers of *Anemone blanda* 'Charmer' make a wonderful companion for the rich blue-purple pansy.

Hot and fiery

Being refined is all very well, but what about when you want passion? Use wallflowers (*Erysimum*) and red and orange tulips to turn up the heat and warm the whole garden.

Tulips do very well in pots and look particularly good when paired with low-growing double daisies (*Bellis perennis*); alternatively, use the large-flowered *Anemone coronaria* 'De Caen' or 'St Bridgid', which are big and bright enough for a display on their own. For a really scorching display, pick a scarlet-red tulip such as 'Apeldoorn' and underplant it with *Bellis perennis* 'Galaxy Red' or 'Habanero'. If your courage fails you, choose a Lily-flowered tulip, which will look more elegant – 'Mariette' is a rich pink. Bicolours can also be more reserved: 'Queen of Sheba' is red with orange margins and 'Red Spring Green' has just enough green to cool the whole flower down.

When choosing pots to go with fiery displays, you can either add more colour with brightly glazed or terracotta containers or, if you're worried your display might be over the top, tone it down with cream or pale green matching pots.

Versatile violas

If you're not sure what colours to use, get some inspiration from the pansies and violas always on sale at garden centres. Familiar to all of us, these little plants can seem rather commonplace. However, they're among the hardest-working in the garden and you can find them in flower all year round, including late winter and early spring, when they really come into their own in pots and other containers.

Violas are available in almost every colour and in several sizes, so there is something for everyone: if the large-flowered, bright-coloured varieties are too brash for you, look for one of the many smaller violas in gentle pastel shades. Use them as under-planting for bulbs, or fill whole pots with single colours or a mixture. At this time of the year, no one is going to criticize you for a lack of colour coordination. (*See also* pages 61, 77–8, 91.)

More combinations

BRIGHT AND CHEERY SCHEME
Anemone blanda
Myosotis sylvatica
Narcissus 'Hawera'
Viola 'Matrix Citrus Mix'

SUBTLE AND ELEGANT SCHEME
Bellis perennis 'The Pearl'
Crocus 'Snow Bunting'
Hyacinthus orientalis 'Jan Bos'
Iris reticulata 'Harmony'
Primula 'Primlet Pink Shades'

HOT AND FIERY SCHEME
Bellis perennis 'Pomponette Red'
Primula polyanthus
Tulipa 'Generaal de Wet'
Tulipa 'Ile de France'

Containers for summer

Summer is a time of abundance, with plants smothered in blooms and foliage – so why do we want containers full of yet more? Well, it seems we all have a soft spot for summer bedding; even gardeners who don't include annuals in their flower beds weaken at the thought of petunias and lobelias trailing from a hanging basket or argyranthemums gracing an urn. At this time of year we simply can't have too much colour.

Traditional mixtures

There's no shortage of flowers for summer colour. In fact, there is such a huge selection of plants around, it can be hard to decide on a colour scheme. This is probably why the bit-of-everything container remains so popular.

Traditional summer displays usually consist of upright 'feature' plants, such as pelargoniums, large-flowered begonias and fuchsias, which tend to sit in the middle of a pot. Around the container edges tumble petunias, sprays of lobelias, bidens and verbena. In between are the spreading plants, such as busy lizzies (*Impatiens*), isotomas, pansies and diascias; there might even be room for a foliage plant or two.

Mixing a variety of summer-flowering plants in a single container can be very successful, especially if you aim for a particular effect, rather than simply choosing a few plants you like the look of. Think about how the colours will work together, and remember to consider the plants' textures and growth habits. (*See also* pages 14–16 and 40–1.)

This simple planting makes the most of the lovely sculptural quality of *Aeonium arboreum* 'Zwartkop'.

Cool combinations

If you want to avoid the jolly-mixture-of-colours approach, try selecting some cool shades, which will give your containers an air of elegance. A combination of whites, pale blues and soft blue-pinks will enliven a patio or quiet corner without taking attention from other parts of the garden. Verbenas come in many just off-white shades and there are the dainty, white-flowered bacopas. The silver-leaved helichrysum would keep the temperature down, but for gentle warmth you could use pale pink busy lizzies or fuchsias. There are also begonias in retiring shades, and lovely powder-blue ageratums.

Restrained use of colour and clever layering has resulted in a stunning window-box display. Plants include nicotiana, ivy, helichrysum and violas.

Warm and hot combinations

The warm shades from the colour wheel – red, orange and yellow – will bring a sense of heat and summer sunshine, even on a cloudy day, to container plantings, and are ideal for enlivening a patio, balcony or wall. For real fire choose brick red, magenta and bright orange, or for gentler warmth select blood red and peachy and apricot hues.

Pelargoniums are available in classic red shades, as are begonias and busy lizzies. Many marigolds (*Tagetes*) are a strong orange colour, and pretty oranges are also available from mimulus and calceolaria, both of which are rather neglected but lovely plants with plenty of charm. Calceolaria has odd, balloon-like flowers that appear strangely solid, while mimulus look a little as if they're sticking their tongues out, which probably accounts for their common name of monkey flower. Gazanias, gaillardias and zinnias are also available in some pretty shocking shades. They look good combined with other plants or on their own.

Zonal, regal and ivy-leaved pelargoniums in hot, bright colours jostle for space and attention on this front door step. The urn lends a certain formality to the scheme.

A touch of class

A good way of creating a strong, coherent display while using lots of plants is to select a classy container, such as a simple stone urn. With a strong form to underpin the show, you can be as inventive as you like with the plants you put in. This is a ploy used in formal gardens, where the symmetrical lines of hedges and paths fool you into thinking everything is restrained and orderly and allows your brain to register the wildly exuberant pot of annuals at the end of a vista without thinking it out of place. Popular choices for such a container include brachyscome, bacopa, helichrysum, ageratum and petunias. Silvers, pinks and white usually abound, but spots of more vivid colour can also be used.

Keeping it simple

Less is often more when it comes to planting containers. One of the best ways to create a striking display is to have a single plant in a simple pot. You can have just one on its own to provide a striking focal point, place a pair either side of a door to mark an entrance, or position several up a flight of steps or side by side along a path or patio edge to highlight an area or boundary and add a splash of colour to hard surfaces. A classic scheme might be a row of terracotta pots each holding a scarlet-flowered pelargonium or a white marguerite.

If you'd like to create an elegant look but can't quite resist growing a selection of plants, you can have matching pots filled with alternating colours of one type of plant – for instance, pelargoniums in red, pink and white; or try grading colours of busy lizzies, so they fade to white from rich cerise.

Another idea is to alternate plants with the same flower colour: for example, a pink busy lizzie and pink argyranthemum or red pelargonium and red begonia and so on. The different flower shapes will create a subtle sense of variety.

A traditional combination of fuchsias and trailing verbena looks wonderful in this bowl-shaped planter. Set on a table, it can be enjoyed closer to eye-level.

Foliage schemes

If you're feeling adventurous, fill containers with a single foliage plant, such as the feathery silver *Senecio cineraria* 'Silver Dust', the grassy *Stipa tenuissima* or one of the many coleus (*Solenostemon*) varieties.

Coleus are known for their vibrant leaf variegations; for a really elegant effect, select one with a simple leaf colour, such as deep purple with a thin green edge, or lime green with a red splash – there are also much more outrageous types available.

A simple combination of foliage and flowers also works very well. Senecio looks wonderful with the latest black-flowered petunia ('Black Velvet'), while the purple-leaved trailing plant *Ipomoea* 'Black Tone' makes a superb underplanting for a red-flowered pelargonium. Silvery lotus is an excellent alternative and also goes well with argyranthemum or osteospermum.

Summer window boxes

When choosing plants for window boxes, consider whether you want to disguise the sides of the box or not. If you have an attractive container, you could highlight the sides with just a couple of strands of a delicate trailing plant, such as helichrysum, but if you want to hide them, create a dense curtain of cover using dichondra or larger-leaved plants such as glechoma.

The slim, rectangular shape of window boxes lends itself to formal plantings – such as a row of grasses or neat, clipped box balls. Herbs are good candidates too, and you can try a formal display of alternating parsley and chives or purple-leaved and green-leaved basil.

Window boxes are also linked with massed planting of a single variety: the classic is ivy-leaved pelargonium cascading from window boxes on Swiss chalet balconies. If you have window boxes on two sills, it's fun to try mirror-image planting, and

Subtle combinations can be created using several shades of the same colour, such as this fresh yellow display of osteospermum, lantana and sanvitalia.

For this imaginative window box, meadow grasses and native flowers have been used to create a delicate, wildlife-friendly display.

This two-tier hanging basket combination of *Petunia* 'Tumbelina Cherry Ripple' and white bacopa is both exuberant and refined.

Flowers of different sizes in shades of pink and cerise fill this rustic-style, wickerwork hanging basket. Petunias and isotoma predominate.

you're most likely to carry it off if you use plants with soft, billowing shapes which will disguise any discrepancies, such as petunias, large-flowered begonias, felicia, calibrachoas and argyranthemums.

Using hanging baskets

Hanging basket plantings are most often informal, the main idea being to have a full basket bursting with a selection of colourful plants. For example, you might include one or two upright plants, such as argyranthemums, pelargoniums and fuchsias, for the top and several spreading and trailing plants for around the rim and to insert into the

Don't forget

Some mail-order companies sell colour-coordinated groups of plants specifically for hanging baskets, which can be useful if you're looking for something in a hurry.

sides: lobelia, petunia, calibrachoa, bidens, bacopa and verbena are a few of the possibilities (*see also* pages 40–1). This should result in a riot of colour throughout summer.

If you wish, you could introduce an air of formality by planting a few matching baskets or by limiting your plant choice or colour scheme. Having several matching baskets, even if they contain madly riotous plantings, will always look more balanced and elegant than just one, while a basket filled with only one colour of petunias, for instance, can look very refined. Using foliage plants is another option. A dark foliage scheme might have *Oxalis triangularis* or *Perilla frutescens* on the top with several *Ipomoea* 'Black Tone' plants trailing down the sides.

Finally, give some thought to the container itself. There are plenty of attractive hanging containers made

from rustic woven hazel or willow, ironwork and terracotta, all of which provide instant structure and can be made formal or informal depending on the planting.

This elegant, sophisticated hanging basket contains just two plant varieties: a bronze-leaved heuchera and a yellow-flowered pansy.

Summer container schemes

Planting containers is easy and fun, but because there's so much choice, it can be difficult to decide on the plants to use and to know which ones go well together. The ideas on these pages are intended to help you to make those decisions. Below you'll see a variety of suggestions for how to arrange plants in the most common containers. Opposite there are combinations showing several of the colour palettes that are possible with bedding – some warm and vibrant, others cool and restful; think about the colour of the pot, too. Don't panic if you can't find the recommended plants; just choose something similar. In containers almost anything goes – don't be scared to have your own ideas.

KEY to symbols

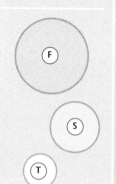

Include a mixture of plant sizes, shapes and growth habits in your container displays.

F = Feature plant, the tall 'star' of the display.

S = Spreading plant, which fills gaps between the feature plants.

T = Trailing plant, which cascades down the sides of the container.

Round-rimmed pot

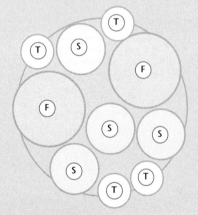

This diagram shows a planting layout for a round-rimmed pot with a diameter of 35–40cm (14–16in), but the layout is also suitable for an urn, a half-barrel, or other similar container. If your pot is bigger, you'll obviously need to add more plants – but don't be tempted to overfill the pot. Begin by increasing the number of trailing plants, then perhaps add another upright or two. If the container you want to use is shallow and so won't hold much compost, it is sensible to drop some plants; using water-retaining crystals is also recommended (*see* page 49).

Hanging basket

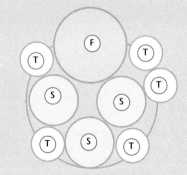

A plan for an open-sided hanging basket with a diameter of 30cm (12in) is shown here; for smaller or larger baskets, reduce or increase the number of plants. With most hanging baskets you want to hide the container completely and this means planting trailers through holes in the sides. However, decorative baskets may not have these holes, in which case you need fewer plants.

Window box

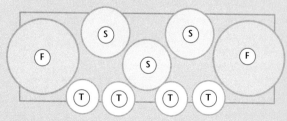

More than with any other type of container, when planting a window box you'll need to think about which side you want the plants to be viewed from – place taller plants at the rear, and trailing ones at the sides and towards the front. This planting layout is for a window box 60cm (24in) long, which is a fairly typical size for a window ledge.

Subtle pinks and silver

Bicoloured fuchsia flowers give you two choices for colour coordination. In this mix, the soft magenta of the fuchsia's 'skirt' ties in nicely with the darker veins in the petunia, while its pale pink 'top' is picked up by the busy lizzie (*Impatiens*).

1 Pink and magenta fuchsia (*F.* 'Lena') (**F**)

2 Soft-pink busy lizzie (*Impatiens walleriana* 'Athena') (**S**)

3 Rich-pink nemesia (*N.* 'Aromatica Rose Pink') (**S**)

4 Pink petunia (*P.* 'Reflection Mix') (**S/T**)

5 Silver foliage (*Dichondra* 'Silver Falls') (**T**)

Cool, watery blues

There are so many shades of blue and most go very well together. Here, the lobelia and petunia are quite dark, emphasizing the pale sky-blue of the felicia. White verbena and variegated leaves add highlights.

1 Sky-blue felicia (*F. amelloides* 'Variegata') (**F**)

2 Violet-blue petunia (*P.* 'Easy Wave Blue') (**S/T**)

3 White verbena (*V.* 'Quartz Silver') (**S/T**)

4 Variegated foliage (*Glechoma hederacea* 'Variegata') (**T**)

5 Dark blue lobelia (*L. erinus* 'Sapphire') (**T**)

Vibrant harmonies

Bright flowers and foliage create a striking, cheerful combination. The daisy-like form of the osteospermums is echoed by the sanvitalias, while the rich orange of the diascias picks up the red of the marigolds.

1 Yellow osteospermum with a hint of pink (*O.* 'Serenity Lemonade') (**F**)

2 Orange diascia (*D.* 'Wink Orange') (**S**)

3 Red marigold (*Tagetes* 'Bonanza Harmony') (**S**)

4 Yellow sanvitalia (*S. procumbens*) (**S/T**)

5 Golden foliage (*Helichrysum petiolare* 'Limelight') (**S/T**)

Chic black and white

White flowers and dark foliage complement each other, sharpening their outlines and intensifying their effect. The daisy-like marguerite lightens the mood, which might otherwise be rather sombre.

1 White marguerite (*Argyranthemum frutescens*) (**F**)

2 Black foliage (*Ophiopogon planiscapus* 'Nigrescens') (**S**)

3 White euphorbia (*E.* 'Diamond Frost') (**S**)

4 White bacopa (*B.* 'Snowflake') (**S/T**)

5 Black foliage (*Ipomoea* 'Black Tone') (**S/T**)

Regal reds and blues

In this rich mix, the blue flowers prevent the red ones from being overpowering while also creating a pleasing contrast. The purple foliage accentuates all the other colours.

1 Dark red tuberhybrida begonia (*B.* 'Nonstop Deep Red') (**F**)

2 Red-purple-leaved oxalis (*O. triangularis*) (**S**)

3 Scarlet verbena (*V.* 'Quartz Scarlet') (**S/T**)

4 Pale blue lobelia (*L.* 'Waterfall Azure Mist') (**T**)

5 Violet-blue calibrachoa (*C.* 'Cabaret Lavender') (**T**)

Soft harmonies

This drought-tolerant planting is suitable for a sunny spot where the leaf colours will catch the light. The silver and blue-grey foliage balances out the sweetness of the pinks, while the purple adds a touch of class.

1 Rich-pink osteospermum (*O.* 'Serenity Pink Improved') (**F**)

2 Pink ptilotus (*P. exaltatus* 'Joey') (**S**)

3 Silver foliage (*Senecio cineraria* 'Silver Dust') (**S**)

4 Blue-grey foliage (*Lotus berthelotii*) (**S/T**)

5 Dark purple-blue verbena (*V.* 'Aztec Blue Velvet') (**S/T**)

Containers for autumn and winter

There's no need to empty pots and store them behind the shed at the end of summer. The key to a colourful autumn and winter is to keep changing container displays. Admittedly, the choice is more restricted than in summer, but any plant that attracts your attention with flowers, fruit, autumn colours or evergreen leaves deserves to be cherished at this time of the year.

Continuous colour

In early autumn there are still quite a lot of flowers around to enable you to create beautiful containers, but you do need to be prepared for their disappearance. A good plan is to plant some permanent containers with evergreen foliage specimens, of which there are plenty (*see* pages 86–91), and have a regularly changing display of smaller feature plants in pots ranged around them.

If you're short of space, plant the back of a container with evergreens and leave some room at the front for a couple of smaller plants. Use cyclamen or small chrysanthemums in the autumn and, as they fade, replace them with heaths (*Erica*), an ornamental cabbage or winter-flowering violas. Later, slip in a few bulbs for flowering in early spring. This way you always have something to look at for very little effort. If you

In this impressive winter container, *Skimmia reevesiana* dominates with its red berries, dramatically set off by the yellow acorus leaves and pink gaultheria berries.

want more colour at any time, you can always use dried fruit or flowers and spray-painted twigs and branches, or even include small garden ornaments.

Clipped and shaped foliage plants are excellent for permanent colour where space is limited. They are perfect for placing either side of a door or at the top or bottom of steps. A single specimen can make an eye-catching focal point at the end of a path. Small Japanese maples (*Acer*) do well in pots and have attractive autumn foliage.

Autumn to winter colour

If you want to create a warm and welcoming autumn display and complement autumn foliage colours, choose red, orange or rust-coloured dahlias and bronze or yellow chrysanthemums; put them in pale clay pots or those with light-coloured glazes to offset their bright

The dark foliage of this black-leaved bugle (*Ajuga*) creates a strong backdrop for other foliage plants and sedum in this autumn container.

This warm bronze-orange cactus-flowered dahlia looks delightful in a terracotta pot, which matches its colour beautifully.

colours. Dahlias look good on their own, while chrysanthemums are somewhat bulbous in outline, so are better with companions to soften their shapes. Both plants also come in strong pinks and mauves, which will create a more contrasting effect with autumn leaves.

As autumn gives way to winter, you need to look harder for flowers, but an excellent compromise is *Skimmia japonica* 'Magic Marlot'. One of several skimmias that have been bred to combat our winter blues, this has white buds in autumn and winter, darkening to red before opening to white flowers in spring.

There are also plenty of warm foliage colours for pots. The

The low-growing bugle *Ajuga* 'Braunherz' makes a wonderful partner for the upright flower spikes of *Calluna vulgaris* 'Garden Girls Pink Alicia'.

More combinations

EVERGREEN FOLIAGE SCHEME
Ajuga reptans 'Black Scallop'
Juniperus communis 'Compressa'
Helichrysum italicum
Heuchera 'Peach Flambé'

AUTUMN SCHEME
Calluna vulgaris Garden Girls series
Chrysanthemum 'Lynn'
Coprosma repens 'Pacific Night'
Heuchera 'Plum Pudding'

MIDWINTER SCHEME
Chamaecyparis lawsoniana 'Ellwoodii'
Festuca glauca 'Elijah Blue'
Hedera helix 'Eva'
Helleborus niger
Viola

WINTER-TO-SPRING SCHEME
Cupressus macrocarpa 'Goldcrest'
Iris 'Harmony'
Narcissus 'Jetfire'
Ophiopogon planiscapus 'Nigrescens'
Primula Bonneli series

coprosmas, such as *Coprosma repens* 'Pacific Night', are not very hardy but have brilliant red-and-purple-tinged, small leaves that look stunning with other foliage plants. Also well worth investigating are the leucothoes, such as 'Scarletta', which has bronze-red leaves, or 'Lovita', which is similar but produces white, scented flowers in spring. Both have attractive spring foliage, too.

Brightening winter gloom

In midwinter, when light levels are at their lowest and draining plants of colour, pale-coloured foliage plants with strong forms and interesting textures are very welcome. Try to combine rounded and upright shapes with trailing and spreading ones. *Euonymus japonicus* 'Pierrolino' has lovely white-variegated young

foliage, or you can use grasses or sedges, such as *Carex oshimensis* 'Evergold'. For a subtler show that relies more on shapes and textures, choose *Carex comans* 'Bronze Form'.

Pale-flowered winter heathers, such as *Erica carnea* f. *albiflora* 'Springwood White' or the lime-leaved 'Golden Starlet', are good for brightening dark areas. If you really want a splash of colour, there is always the intriguing ornamental cabbage, which comes in shades of pink and purple. It looks good planted singly or in groups in pots and lasts for weeks.

Don't forget

Garden centres often sell plants such as camellias in pots just as they're coming into bloom. They look lovely, but need attention to keep healthy in a pot.

Planting and growing

If you're new to gardening, growing and caring for annuals and tender perennials is a great way to take your first steps into what is a fascinating and absorbing hobby. Most of these plants grow fast and flower well under a range of conditions, and you'll quickly learn the basics of plant care. Inevitably, as well as amazing successes you will have failures; however, as the plants are intended only for short-term display, this is not as disastrous or expensive as if they were permanent garden residents.

Starting out

Even if you're aiming for only a few weeks of colour in summer, you'll need to invest in a basic set of good-quality garden tools. When it comes to obtaining plants, you can either sow seed (*see* pages 46–8) or, for instant impact, buy pot-grown plants that can be put straight into borders or containers.

A standard trowel (left) is essential for planting bedding. The slimline type is useful for smaller containers.

What you'll need

A good-quality spade and fork are essential if you're planting bedding in the garden. A trowel is also vital, and you'll need a garden rake for sowing seeds and levelling flower beds. A good pair of secateurs is useful for dead-heading and general tidying, as is a small hand fork or lightweight hoe for weeding. Other handy items include a watering can, some gardening gloves and, in a large garden, a wheelbarrow for carting compost and plants.

Buying plants

The first step to growing bedding plants successfully is to buy healthy specimens in the first place. They should be short and stocky, with plenty of leaves and buds. Tiny plants that are already in flower are often 'stressed' and won't continue to flower for long. Today, plants tend to be grown in individual cells rather than in trays, because they don't suffer root disturbance when being transplanted, so there is no check in growth and they establish easily once in their final position. They are available in a variety of containers of different sizes.

Plugs These are smallish plants, available either individually or in packs by mail order and in garden centres and nurseries. They're economical and a great way to obtain a lot of one variety.

Plugs can be planted directly into decorative containers, such as hanging baskets. Give them plenty of room to develop and allow them a week or two to put down new roots before hardening them off (*see* page 47) and displaying them. Plugs destined for beds and borders need to be planted into bigger pots and allowed to grow larger before they're hardened off and planted out.

Multi-cell packs Larger plants are sold in garden centres in plastic modular trays. Each cell contains a single plant and the number of cells can be anything between four and 40, although six is standard. The plants can be put straight into the garden or decorative containers, provided the conditions are right.

Individual pots Larger, more mature bedding plants are sold, often in flower, in individual pots starting at about 9cm (3½in). This is perhaps the best way to buy a single plant or a few feature plants, such as pelargoniums, begonias or fuchsias. The smallest are good value, but prices increase with pot size and larger ones are relatively expensive.

Bedding plant containers

Bedding plants are sold in a range of containers according to their stage of growth. Below are some of the most common examples available in the shops and online.

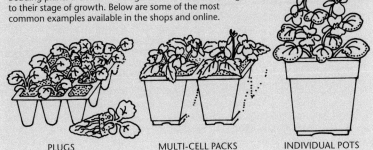

PLUGS   MULTI-CELL PACKS   INDIVIDUAL POTS

Plant names

The names of annuals can vary depending on the seed sellers or plant grower concerned. Those given in this book are as accurate as possible, but if you see something with a very similar name it is almost certainly the same plant or a close version of it.

Sowing and planting

Most annuals are very easy to raise from seed, and for some that will be the only option available (these plants are highlighted in the directory, pages 56–91). However, some are tricky to get to germinate and can need extra warmth (*see* lower box, opposite). In this case, it might be better to buy them as young plants. Biennials and tender perennials are also easier to grow from plants. Bulbs are best bought when dormant, although you can buy them growing in pots.

Sowing seeds of annuals in containers

Sowing seeds into containers is usually the most assured way of getting plenty of plants. However, some annuals dislike disturbance and these are best sown straight into their final positions (*see* page 48).

Instructions on sowing seed and germination times should be given on the seed packet. Some seed will be labelled 'F₁ hybrids', which means the plant breeder has crossed two stable seed lines, resulting in particularly vigorous, healthy plants. F_1 seed is more costly but more vigorous than other types of seed.

Sowing seeds

Most seeds are sown in seed trays or small pots, as shown here. You'll need to fill the container with loamless (also called soilless) seed or potting compost. Seed composts usually contain small, white particles, which are vermiculite or perlite; these are lightweight, inert additives that help drainage and aeration, important for all plants.

If you're sowing particularly large seeds, put one or two into individual 7cm (3in) pots or seed modules. For tiny seeds, scatter them thinly over the surface of a seed tray, then cover them with a thin layer of compost; alternatively, mix the seed with very fine sand and scatter it over the surface of the compost.

Now put the containers in a suitable place for germination, such as a light windowsill with a steady temperature of around 15–21°C (60–70°F). Generally, most seeds take between one and three weeks.

Pricking out seedlings

Once the seed germinates, and the first 'seed' leaves have appeared, the seedlings need to be transplanted to allow them to grow on. Carefully

HOW TO sow seeds

1 Fill a small pot or seed tray with fresh seed compost and gently firm and level the surface. Scatter the seeds evenly and thinly across the surface. Larger seeds can be individually placed. Avoid letting any of the seeds touch each other, since they will restrict each other's growth.

2 Sieve or sprinkle a thin layer of compost over the seeds. You can use vermiculite or perlite instead. Generally, small seeds need to be just covered, but larger ones should have a deeper layer over them. Stand the pots or trays in tepid water until the surface of the compost is damp.

3 Place the pots or trays in a well-lit position, but not in full sun. Putting them inside plastic bags reduces water evaporation and temperature fluctuations, so may assist with germination.

4 Check the pots daily, watering sparingly if they are dry. Remove the bags when the seedlings appear. Once the 'seed' leaves are large enough to handle, transplant them singly to give them more space.

prise out the seedlings and insert them into a compost-filled seed tray, spacing them about 3.5cm (1½in) apart. Set the seedlings so the seed leaves are a little closer to the surface than they were before. Handle them by their leaves, not the stems. When the roots have extended (after about six weeks), you can transfer the plants into individual pots filled with fresh potting compost. Most bedding plants, though, will have sufficient space if they stay in their trays until they're planted out.

Hardening off

Seedlings that have been raised indoors (including young plants from the garden centre) will need time to adjust gradually to the conditions outside before they're planted into the garden.

Wait for a spell of warm, still weather, then place the plants in a sheltered site outdoors during the day but bring them indoors at night. You'll need to do this for about a week or so, depending on the weather. Then start leaving the plants out overnight. If the weather deteriorates, be ready to protect them until it improves again.

Planting out

Most bedding needs planting out after all danger of frost is past. Fork over the soil, make a hole for each plant, and put the plant in position; the top of the rootball should be level with the soil surface. Backfill with soil around the roots, firm it in gently and water well. (For planting up containers, *see* pages 49–50).

Early planting and sowing

Biennial wallflowers (*Erysimum*) must be planted in autumn so that they can establish for early flowering.

Some hardy annuals, including sweet peas (*Lathyrus*) and *Clarkia*, can also be sown in the autumn. The benefit is that they will have a strong root system by the following spring. They may also flower slightly sooner than spring-sown specimens. Sweet peas are usually sown in pots, while *Clarkia* are sown directly into the garden. Both will need protection during very cold weather, and you should check them regularly to ensure they aren't being eaten by pests.

Propagators and cold frames

If you're planning on growing lots of seeds, it's well worth considering buying a propagator and a cold frame, both of which can be obtained quite cheaply. Even a very basic unheated propagator gives your seeds a protected environment that can help germination. Some seeds need heat to germinate (it'll say this on the packet), in which case a heated propagator is vital. Place propagators in a position that is well lit but doesn't get direct sun, such as on a windowsill or beside patio doors.

Cold frames are placed outside in a sheltered, semi-shady position and make the perfect halfway house for seedlings that are being hardened off. Lift the lid during the day to acclimatize them and then close it at night.

Plants grown under cover, in a greenhouse or cold frame or on a windowsill, need to be acclimatized slowly to the outside world before being planted out.

1 Fork over and then rake the soil so that it is level and has a fine surface that the seedlings can easily grow through. Use sand to mark areas to be sown.

2 Within each area make several shallow depressions, or drills, using the back of a rake or a bamboo cane. Sow the seeds by sprinkling them thinly along the rows.

3 Cover the seeds with a thin layer of soil, then protect the whole area with twiggy branches to prevent birds and other animals from disturbing them.

Direct sowing

Some annuals are sown 'direct', or *in situ*, in their final positions, mainly because they dislike disturbance. Direct sowing is quicker and easier than raising seeds in pots, and can produce a more natural effect, but the risk of patchy germination and loss of seedlings to slugs and snails is greater, so be prepared to lose some.

Begin by digging over the flower bed thoroughly with a fork, then use a garden rake to create a level surface. It is well worth removing any large stones and other debris. Once you've finished you should have what is called a fine tilth.

If the whole flower bed is going to be sown, mark up the areas for each different type of seed using sand, as shown above. Now you're ready to sow. Use the back of the rake or a bamboo cane to make short, shallow furrows into which you will sow the seeds: even though you're aiming for a natural effect, it always makes good sense to sow the seeds in rows, as this will help you to distinguish them from weeds when they germinate.

Increasing your stock

By collecting seeds and taking cuttings of your (or other people's) bedding plants, you can ensure you hang on to particular favourites as well as saving a bit of money next year.

COLLECTING SEEDS

Many annuals, such as poppies and nasturtiums, produce seed that can be collected for sowing next year, but remember seed collected from hybrids and improved forms will produce variable plants – few will be as good as their parents. Towards the end of the flowering season, allow a few flowers to develop seedheads. Leave these to mature and dry on the plant, then cut them off the plant and shake them out of their pods into paper bags. Label and date the bags and store them in a cool, dry place until the seeds are needed.

TAKING CUTTINGS

Foliage bedding plants, including coleus, ajuga and euonymus, as well as shrubby plants, such as fuchsia and pelargoniums, can be propagated by cuttings, usually in spring or late summer. Choose healthy stems and cut them cleanly just below a leaf joint. They should be about 8cm (3in) long.

Remove the lower leaves, then put the cuttings into pots or seed trays filled with a damp mix of loamless (or soilless) potting compost and sand (about half and half). Roots will form in about four to six weeks.

Seeds for direct sowing

Calendula officinalis

Centaurea cyanus

Clarkia elegans

Consolida ajacis

Eschscholzia californica

Iberis umbellata

Linaria maroccana

Myosotis

Nemophila

Nigella

Papaver rhoeas

Papaver somniferum

Salvia viridis

Tagetes

Tropaeolum (most)

Planting up containers

First, choose a suitable container (*see* page 33); holes in the base are vital in order to prevent the plants' roots from sitting in wet compost, which causes them to rot. Generally, you need a 2.5cm (1in) diameter of drainage hole for every 30cm (12in) pot. Before filling the container with compost, put some crocks (pieces of broken terracotta pot) in the base. As well as reducing the volume of compost you need, this also helps with drainage. If you don't have crocks, use a few small stones or even pieces of polystyrene packing.

Potting composts

For short-term displays, loamless (also called soilless) compost, such as multipurpose compost, is usually ideal. It is lightweight, weed-free and water-retentive. For a long-term display, it's worth using a loam-based (or soil-based) compost. John Innes

Before planting up your containers it is worth doing a trial run to find the most attractive combinations.

No. 2 is a good choice for many plants. Mixing in loamless compost (about half and half) reduces the weight of the pot and increases water-retention and aeration.

Compost additives

If you want more water retention, add some water-retaining crystals. These absorb water and slowly release it back to the plant, making drought less likely. Another valuable addition is slow-release fertilizer. Many loamless composts come with about six weeks' food supply, but adding more helps to ensure your plants get the nutrition they need for a longer period. For added drainage and aeration, use perlite, vermiculite, grit or sand.

Don't forget

Pot feet, which lift the container off the ground, are attractive and help drainage too.

HOW TO plant a basic container

1 Water the plants in their pots. Place some crocks at the base of the container. Mix any additives into your potting compost and half fill the pot with it. Gently ease the plants out of their pots. If they are well anchored, either invert the pot and tap the rim on a firm edge or, if it is flimsy plastic, roll it on its side with your hand.

2 Place the plant in the container, leaving a gap of about 1cm (½in) between the top of the rootball and the rim of the pot. Add or remove compost under the plant to get the position right. Add more plants, filling in the spaces between them with compost as you go. Be prepared to have several attempts to create a good-looking display.

3 Water well, using a watering can with a fine rose. This will rinse spilt compost from the leaves and helps to bed the plants in. Add more compost if necessary. Finally, put a layer of decorative material, such as gravel or pebbles, over the surface of the compost. This keeps weeds down and reduces water evaporation.

HOW TO plant a traditional hanging basket

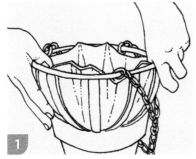

1 Find something to balance the basket on for planting up. A flowerpot or bucket is fine. Line the basket with a suitable liner, pressing it in place.

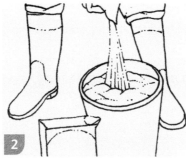

2 Make up your compost mix in a bucket. Put some compost in the bucket, then add pre-soaked water-retaining crystals and some slow-release fertilizer (*see* page 49).

3 Push or tap the plants out of their containers. If they are in trays, separate the plants by pulling them apart carefully to avoid damaging the roots.

4 Make a few holes in the liner with a knife (these are where you'll be putting your trailing plants) and then put some compost in the bottom of the basket.

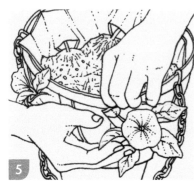

5 Start by planting up the sides, inserting trailing plants through the holes. It is usually easier to push the roots through from the outside. Keep adding compost as you plant the sides.

6 When you reach the top, plant some upright and bushy, spreading plants to complete the display. Add more compost, leaving a small depression in the centre for watering. Water well.

Types of basket

Traditional hanging baskets are made of plastic-coated wire mesh and when they are planted well they make a ball of flowers and foliage, which takes some beating. The idea is to plant through the mesh as well as out of the top (as shown left), so the container itself is entirely hidden. This can be a bit fiddly and needs practice, so you might prefer to use a solid decorative basket. There are plenty around, varying from woven willow to dried heather or even plastic. Narrow your choice by deciding on the sort of display you want and the colours you're going to use beforehand.

Basket liners

Basket liners are essential for open-sided baskets, otherwise the compost will simply fall out. Solid baskets do not need liners. There are various liners available from coir to compressed wood or recycled paper, and most do a very good job. Some will need cutting into shape, but you can also buy basket and liner kits ready made for each other.

How many plants?

When planting up your hanging baskets, do remember that each plant needs space to grow and develop, so limit your numbers. In a 30cm (12in) basket, eight to ten plants are sufficient, although tiny plants, particularly lobelia, may be planted slightly more densely. It may take a while for the plants to spread and disguise the whole basket, but the end result will be much more rewarding than if you stuff the basket full of plants from the start. Most importantly, the plants will last much longer, extending the season of interest, and flower more prolifically, since they won't be fighting for root room or food and water. (For suggested planting layouts, *see* page 40.)

Care and maintenance

When you've planted up your instant-colour garden, you'll need to do a little bit of maintenance to enable the plants to give you their best performance. Most annuals are genetically programmed to produce masses of flowers and then die. Your job is to keep them alive – and looking their best – for as long as possible. Other bedding plants also benefit from regular care and attention.

Watering

Bedding plants require regular, thorough watering, particularly for the first two or three weeks after planting and during dry spells. In the summer, containers have to be watered at least once a day, often even if it has rained; hanging baskets may need two soakings on very hot days. Flower beds can be allowed to dry out a bit between waterings. Use your trowel to see how far the soil has dried out and water if more than the top 5cm (2in) is dry.

Feeding

Plants need food in order to grow healthy leaves and to flower well. When you prepare the garden soil for planting, it's well worth adding a general-purpose granulated or powdered fertilizer. This will provide most of your plants with what they need for the whole of the growing season. However, if they start to show signs of starvation, including yellowing leaves, few flowers or poor growth, at any time, you can give them a liquid feed when you water.

Add slow-release fertilizer pellets to hanging baskets to ensure the inmates get all the nutrients they require.

Containers need weekly feeding because the plants' roots will soon fill the pots and exhaust the food supply that was in the potting compost to begin with. Feed with a liquid fertilizer when you water or put slow-release fertilizer pellets into the compost.

Be aware that some annuals don't need food; in fact, they will produce

Mulching

If your soil is very light and free-draining, you can add a mulch, which will slow water evaporation. A mulch is a bulky layer of organic matter, about 5cm (2in) thick, placed around the plants' stems. Mulches are available in bags from the garden centre and include bark, coir and cocoa shells. Alternatively, you can use home-made compost, leaf mould or well-rotted manure, although these are more likely to grow weeds. Gravel can be used but it's less suitable if you intend to disturb the soil regularly for replanting.

Water newly planted bedding regularly. Soak the soil or compost thoroughly rather than giving a light sprinkling. The water needs to reach the plants' roots.

lots of foliage but fewer flowers if they're in rich soil. The directory, on pages 56–91, tells you about the plants' preferences.

Weeding

No matter how well you've prepared the soil, weeds will appear and they should be removed as soon as possible so that they don't spoil the appearance of your display and affect the growth of your plants. It's particularly important to weed beds that have had seeds sown direct, because the young seedlings will find it hard to compete with weeds.

Use a hoe to decapitate small weeds from around young plants; be very careful not to disturb the plants' roots or damage their stems. Larger weeds are best removed using a hand fork or trowel. Where plants are very close together, it's easiest to scratch the surface with

a hand fork and uproot the weeds before removing them. However, you'll find that weeds are less likely to emerge once your plants have grown together and shaded the soil.

Weeding has another benefit. After planting and watering, the surface of the soil can form a crust that's difficult for water to penetrate. Disturbing the surface during weeding will break up this crust.

Stakes and supports

Tall plants are usually best staked in order to ensure they remain upright, particularly after a heavy shower of rain. Also, climbers must be given something to climb up. Put stakes in place soon after planting, so the plant's growth will hide them. Tie the stems to the stakes using soft twine. For some plants, leafless, twiggy branches, such as prunings from garden shrubs and trees, make good informal supports.

Make a regular habit of tying climbers to their supports. This will prevent them sprawling everywhere and gives you the chance to enjoy the flowers close up.

Regular dead-heading keeps displays looking good and helps to encourage continued flowering.

Pinching out and dead-heading

Pinching out is a quick and simple task that encourages young plants to grow plenty of sideshoots, which means a lot more flowers. It involves removing the growing-tips of the main stems using your fingernails, pinching back to the next set of leaves. You may need to do this several times during summer.

Dead-heading is the process of removing dead flowerheads from plants, by either plucking or snipping them off. Do this as soon as the flower fades, making sure you also take off the old flower stem and any developing seedheads. Not only does this make the display look a lot better but it also ensures that plants keep flowering. Their ambition is to produce seeds, and if you allow them to do this, they don't feel the need to continue flowering.

Lifting tender perennials

Tender perennials can survive year after year if they're lifted and kept in a frost-free place in winter, but few of us have the space to store them. However, tender tuberous plants, such as dahlias, cannas and some begonias (see page 64), can be stored quite easily in a small space.

In mid- to late autumn, dig up the tubers and store them in boxes of very slightly damp sand or potting compost in a frost-free place, such as a shed or garage. Cannas and begonias should be brought in before the first frosts; in the case of dahlias, wait until frost has blackened the foliage. In spring, plant the tubers into large pots and, once they have several strong shoots and there is no further danger of frost, plant them out.

Plant problems and remedies

Annuals and other bedding plants are generally reliable performers that repay a little trouble with plenty of rewards. Provided you plant them in a suitable site and give them adequate food and water, they should thrive. However, like any other plants, they can be attacked by pests and occasionally suffer from diseases. When this is the case, it's best to deal with the problems straightaway. Below are some of the most common problems that affect bedding plants.

Aphids

Plant shoots, young leaves and flower buds may be colonized by aphids, which are usually green (known as greenfly), but may be black, grey, pink or brown. Aphids suck the sap, weakening the plant and distorting its growth. Also, they are the main agents that spread disfiguring virus diseases (*see* page 54), so it's vital to deal with them as soon as possible. Aphids affect most bedding plants, particularly nasturtiums, lupins and poppies.

Prevention and control Keep an eye on your display and catch them early. Do a daily check and gently squash the insects off buds and leaves to keep numbers down. Attract natural predators to the garden – lacewings, ladybirds and hoverflies all prey on aphids. If necessary, spray plants with pyrethrum, soft or insecticidal soap or plant oils.

Caterpillars

Caterpillars are the larvae of butterflies and moths. They eat the

leaves of a wide range of plants, including bedding, and can quickly demolish whole plants if not stopped. Signs of attack are usually irregular holes eaten in the leaves. Caterpillars are particularly fond of nasturtiums and may also be a nuisance on pelargoniums.

Prevention and control If you spot caterpillars on your plants, pick them off and squash them. Look on the undersides of leaves, where you might also see clusters of eggs, which should be removed. Check them at night too, since some caterpillars feed only after dark. For larger numbers use pyrethrum spray or, as a last resort, you could use an approved insecticide. However, it's just as easy to pick off these very visible pests.

Cutworms

These soil-based pests, which are the larvae of moths, are maggot-like and pale brown or green. There is no sign of them above ground, but from early summer onwards they eat through a plant's roots, causing sudden wilting and death of many young plants and seedlings.

Prevention and control As soon as you notice damage, dig about in the surrounding soil to find these pests and squash them.

Damping off

Damping off is a fungal disease that affects seedlings soon after they emerge above the soil. The seeds germinate well and start to grow thickly, but then all of a sudden the stems collapse, causing wilting and death. It is most common in plants growing in seed trays and pots, where a patch of seedlings may die while the rest of them seem to be unaffected. All types of seedlings are susceptible to damping off.

Prevention and control Avoid sowing seeds too thickly and prick out seedlings as soon as possible. Use good-quality compost. Water seeds with fresh tap water, and do not overwater. As a preventative measure, water seedlings with a copper-based fungicide. This will not work if the seedlings have already been infected.

Powdery mildew

This is a fungal disease that grows a white powder coating on the upper surfaces of leaves. The foliage turns yellow and distorted and growth is stunted. Annuals and young plants are most badly affected, especially pansies and pot marigolds.

Prevention and control The most common cause is a combination of dry roots and damp leaves, so pay attention to watering and water the soil rather than the leaves. Mulch the soil to keep it damp. Cut back plants to increase air circulation and don't plant too thickly in future.

Red spider mite

Very active during dry weather, red spider mites infest the undersides of leaves, sucking the sap and making them turn yellow and papery. They are too small to be seen, but you can make out their dusty webs. They affect a huge range of plants.

Prevention and control Keep plants well watered and mist the leaf undersides daily if you spot any signs of red spider mite. Some plants, including morning glory (*Ipomoea*), are particularly susceptible, so mist regularly to prevent the problem in the first place.

Slugs and snails

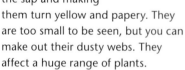

Probably the most destructive of all common garden pests, slugs and snails can see off whole rows of emerging seedlings and cause a lot of damage to young plants. Signs include chewed leaves and stripped foliage. It is worth trying to get on top of the problem before planting in spring. Among the most badly damaged bedding plants are dahlias, lupins and larkspur.

Prevention and control There is a biological control (*Phasmarhabditis hermaphrodita*) that can be used before sowing seeds and just before planting out. Water it onto the soil in warm, damp weather and it will kill slugs for about six weeks. It is not as effective on snails. Go out at night and hand pick these. You need to kill them; if you simply throw them over the garden hedge, they will return!

Beer traps made from jam jars sunk into the ground and filled with beer will catch a few slugs and snails, while copper tape can be used around containers and raised beds; it delivers a little electric shock. Grit can also be used around plants.

Slug pellets are popular. Those made of aluminium sulphate are the most environmentally friendly, or try newer versions made from sheep's wool. Ferric phosphate is effective. Avoid metaldehyde pellets. Clear away dead slugs on a daily basis.

Viruses

Yellow streaking in the leaves, which also become distorted, is the most common symptom of a range of viruses. The plant may be stunted too, and flower poorly, if at all. The most badly affected bedding plants are daffodils, dahlias, gladioli, sweet peas, lilies, lupins, pelargoniums and petunias.

Prevention and control Viruses are spread by aphids and other sap-sucking insects, so it's essential that these pests are kept under control (*see* page 53). Also, weeds may harbour viruses, so keep on top of your weeding. Once a plant is affected by a virus there is no cure, so destroy contaminated plants before the virus spreads.

Other problems that affect bedding plants

COLD DAMAGE
Putting bedding plants out too early or a sudden unexpected cold snap in summer can make leaves turn purple or yellow. If the plant is still alive, nurse it back to health by removing the worst-affected leaves and putting it somewhere more sheltered.

FEW FLOWERS
Overfeeding bedding plants with nitrogen-rich fertilizer will result in too much foliage and too few flowers. Some also dislike deep shade and will stop flowering in shady spots. Cut back on feeding or move plants to a brighter position.

SCORCH MARKS
Watering plants on a sunny day can damage leaves if they become wet; the droplets burn the leaf tissues, producing yellow or brown spots. Water damage on petals can appear as white flecks. Avoid wetting the plant and try to water in the morning or evening.

ANIMAL DAMAGE
Cats, dogs, moles and birds can all dig up new plants. Use twiggy sticks to discourage cats, birds and dogs. You'll need professional help to get rid of moles.

Seasonal tasks

The idea behind an instant colour garden is that you can do it instantly. However, this does depend on you having a garden that is in good shape to begin with. If you want more colour for less money, your best bet is to grow at least some of your plants from seed and plant some things in advance – and that takes forethought. This checklist aims to give you a simple overview of the gardening year with the key tasks you need to undertake in order to have plenty of colour in every season.

Early spring

- Fork over flower borders and remove weeds.
- Buy plug plants for summer displays. Pot them into 8cm (3in) pots, but don't put them outside until all danger of frost has passed.
- Sow seeds of most annuals from now until late spring.
- Plant bulbs such as lilies and gladioli in pots or in the garden.

Mid-spring

- Dead-head daffodils and other bulbs, leaving their leaves to die back naturally (don't cut them back).
- As seedlings grow, thin those in flower beds to recommended spacings. If they're in trays, pot them on individually until they're ready to go into the garden.
- Plant dahlia tubers and other tender perennials in pots for planting out in summer.
- Fill containers with bedding plants, including those purchased as plugs in early spring.
- Begin hardening off all seedlings and plants grown under cover.

Choose a warm, still day to put out bedding plants. Water them before-hand, give them adequate space to grow and water well after planting.

Late spring

- Plant out bedding and bring out hardened-off plants in containers.
- Stake or otherwise support climbers and taller bedding plants.
- Water plants until they're well established. Check containers daily.
- Take cuttings of fuchsias, coleus and other shrubby bedding plants.

Summer

- Dead-head and water plants often.
- Plant out tender perennials raised in pots, or plunge them, pots and all, into flower beds.
- As lilies and other potted bulbs come into flower, plunge them into their allotted places in the garden.
- Remove plants as their flowering season ends and add more.

- Take cuttings of pelargoniums and other plants for next year's displays.
- Pick flowers for drying and for decorative indoor arrangements.
- Sow seed of biennials, such as daisies (*Bellis perennis*), in pots.

Early and mid-autumn

- As bedding plants fade, remove them and fork over flower beds. Add compost to enrich the soil.
- Continue to sow seeds of biennials in pots and sow sweet peas.
- In the garden and in pots plant spring bulbs, such as daffodils and snowdrops. Plant lilies, too.
- In the garden sow seeds of hardy annuals, such as *Clarkia* and *Calendula*.
- Plant wallflowers in the garden.
- Plant autumn and winter containers with evergreen foliage and fruiting plants as well as heathers and cyclamen.

Late autumn

- Dig up dahlias, cannas and other tender tuberous perennials for overwintering. Store the tubers in very slightly damp sand or potting compost in a frost-free place.
- Plant tulip and hyacinth bulbs.
- Add winter-flowering pansies and primulas to containers and borders.

Winter

- Dead-head winter-flowering bedding plants; you may still need to water now and again.
- Protect outdoor pots in bubble wrap in frosty conditions.
- Wash empty pots in warm, soapy water or disinfectant before storing them indoors over winter.
- Order seed and plug plants online and from mail-order catalogues.

Recommended bedding plants

Bedding is big business. The number of plants available increases by hundreds each year – which also means that some varieties are superseded by others that flower better or have improved resistance to disease. This directory features a good cross-section of the plants available. Many come in a wide range of colours, so if you don't like the colour shown, remember that there are sure to be others you can choose from. The directory is organized by season, but bear in mind that flowers can often appear earlier or continue to perform later than indicated – and, of course, that foliage plants have a much longer period of interest.

About this directory

The plants in this directory will all provide wonderful seasonal colour in flower beds or container displays. Unless otherwise specified, they are either annuals or perennials grown as annuals (*see* pages 9–11). The main season of interest for annuals is the summer, so the rest of the year it is chiefly other plants, such as bulbs and shrubs, that provide the colour. Most plants listed are widely sold as growing plants in pots and will provide instant colour. However, some are available as bulbs only, and where 'grow from seed' is specified, sowing seed may be the only option. A list of those usually sown direct, or *in situ*, is given on page 48. In the case of trees and shrubs, the heights provided refer to the size of plants in pots rather than the eventual height reached when in the open ground. For plants for particular uses, effects and conditions, *see* pages 20–3.

KEY to symbols

In this chapter the following symbols are used to indicate a plant's preferred growing conditions and uses. Each plant's height (H) is given, but in the case of trailers height means drop.

Unless otherwise specified, plants are fully hardy and prefer well-drained, reasonably fertile soil that rarely dries out.

- ○ Prefers/tolerates an open, sunny site
- ◑ Prefers/tolerates some shade
- ● Prefers/tolerates full shade
- ✻ Will survive winter in a sheltered site
- ✿ Always needs protection from frost
- pH↓ Prefers neutral to acidic soil
- pH↑ Prefers neutral to alkaline soil
- ✂ Good for cut flowers
- ❖ Season of main interest

Spring

Early in the year, most flowering plants are bulbs, but there are some biennials and perennials, too. The flowers often last only a few weeks, but many are brightly colourful, bringing a welcome cheer to the still-sleeping garden.

Anemone blanda 'Blue Shades'
○ ◑ ❖ SPRING
H 15cm (6in)

With its rich blue, daisy flowers and delicate foliage, this little corm is an attractive companion for bright yellow daffodils and variously coloured crocuses. Grow in pots or to fill gaps in borders. Varieties are available in white ('White Splendour') and pink ('Pink Star'). Look out for packs of corms in mixed colours.

Anemone coronaria
○ ❖ SPRING
H 30–40cm (12–16in)

This bulb has large flowers in a range of shades including rich and dark colours, unusual for the time of year. De Caen Group is a collective name given to the single-flowered varieties of which 'Mister Fokker' (shown above) is blue; St Bridgid Group are doubles. It is best in containers or at the front of flower beds. Plant it with crocuses, small irises and among evergreen foliage plants.

Bellis perennis Double daisy
○ ◑ ❖ LATE WINTER to SUMMER
H 8–15cm (3–6in)

A double-flowered relative of our native daisy, this biennial has so many petals that the flowers look like small pompons. It is available in single shades including pink ('Bellissima Rose', shown above) and white ('The Pearl') and mixes, such as 'Tasso' (red, white and pink). Use it as a foil for tulips or to complement crocuses and irises, at the front of borders or in pots.

Crocus 'Snow Bunting'
○ ◑ ❖ LATE WINTER to EARLY SPRING
H 8–10cm (3–4in)

The pretty, creamy-white blooms of this tiny bulb open towards the very end of winter, making it among the first flowers of spring. Plant it with pale-coloured primulas and early daffodils or put it in pots on a wall or outdoor table so the delicate petals can be appreciated.

Crocus vernus 'Pickwick'
Dutch crocus
○ ◑ ✻ SPRING
H 10–12cm (4–5in)

Bright orange stigmas contrast beautifully with the heavily purple-and-white-striped flowers of this bulb. Its colouring makes it particularly effective for contrasting with low-growing daffodils such as *Narcissus* 'Jumblie' or 'Jetfire', but it also looks good planted *en masse* on its own, either in pots or in flower beds close to the house.

Dianthus Sunflor series
○ ◑ pH↑✗✻ MID-SPRING to AUTUMN
H 10–15cm (4–6in)

Bred for a long flowering season, these perennial pinks are compact with plenty of healthy foliage. The flowers, some of which are scented, come in many shades including 'Allura' (pink), 'Citrien' (pale yellow) and 'Margarita' (dark crimson and white, shown above). Grow in containers or with other low-level bedding, such as pansies and double daisies (*Bellis perennis*) or evergreen foliage plants, at the front of borders.

Erysimum 'Bowles's Mauve'
Perennial wallflower
○ pH↑✻ SPRING to SUMMER
H 60–75cm (24–30in)

With its upright, rich-mauve flowers and grey-green leaves, this bushy evergreen wallflower can be used as a shrub for a sunny border or in pots. Try combining it with tulips or other perennial wallflowers, such as 'Sweet Sorbet' or 'Bredon'. Perennial wallflowers can be kept for a few years, but most become scruffy and leggy. They propagate easily from late-summer or autumn cuttings.

Erysimum cheiri Wallflower
○ pH↑✻ SPRING to EARLY SUMMER
H 20–50cm (8–20in)

Popular varieties of the sweet-scented biennial wallflower include 'Persian Carpet Mixed' and the red-orange 'Fire King' (shown above), an excellent companion for similarly coloured tulips or for a purple-flowered variety, such as *Tulipa* 'Queen of Night'. It also looks good with forget-me-nots and double daisies (*Bellis perennis*). Plant it near paths and seating areas for the scent.

Fritillaria meleagris
Snakeshead fritillary
○ ✻ SPRING
H 25cm (10in)

This is a classy bulb with delicately marked, dusky purple flowers hanging from the top of slender stems; it is also available in white. It is often seen growing *en masse* in grass, but looks good in an early-spring container with small daffodils, pale primulas, *Anemone blanda* or small evergreen foliage plants, such as *Euonymus fortunei* 'Emerald Gaiety' or the ivy *Hedera helix* 'Eva'.

Hyacinthus orientalis Hyacinth
○ ◑ ✗✻ LATE WINTER to EARLY SPRING
H 20–30cm (8–12in)

Hyacinths come with single or double flowers in a range of colours and most with a lovely fragrance. Widely available varieties include 'Ostara' (violet, shown above), 'Jan Bos' (cerise) and 'City of Haarlem' (pale yellow) – all single-flowered. Hyacinths are traditionally grown on their own in groups in containers or border edges. However, they look good with other spring bulbs, particularly daffodils, and violas.

Iris 'Harmony'

○ pH ↓ ❖ LATE WINTER to EARLY SPRING
H 12–15cm (5–6in)

This bulbous plant, with its royal-blue flowers, belongs to the Reticulata Group of irises, which are mostly spring-flowering and small with sculptural blooms, usually in shades of blue or violet with yellow and often white markings. Grow it in a group in a bowl or with snowdrops, daffodils and primulas. Similar varieties include the darker 'Joyce', and 'George', which is rich maroon-purple.

Iris 'Katharine Hodgkin'

○ pH ↓ ❖ LATE WINTER to EARLY SPRING
H 12–15cm (5–6in)

A bulbous plant belonging to the Reticulata Group of irises, 'Katharine Hodgkin' differs from most in that its small, shapely flowers are very pale, almost white, with heavy, dark blue markings. Its pale colour works well with a dark foil provided by, say, *Ophiopogon planiscapus* 'Nigrescens', *Ajuga reptans* 'Atropurpurea' or even the foliage of cyclamen. It can also be grown in a pot alone or with small daffodils.

Myosotis sylvatica 'Victoria Blue'
Forget-me-not

○ ◐ ❖ SPRING to EARLY SUMMER
H 15cm (6in)

This dwarf variety has flowers of an unusually dark blue, which emphasizes the bright yellow centres. The archetypal spring flower, forget-me-nots go well with almost any other spring-flowering plant in containers and garden borders. Forget-me-nots are biennial and will self-seed freely. To avoid this, pull them out before seeding, but do allow a few to set seed – they are easy to remove where they aren't wanted.

Narcissus 'February Gold'

○ ◐ ✗ ❖ EARLY SPRING
H 30cm (12in)

This is one of the earliest daffodils, producing nodding flowers of a rich golden yellow. It is a particularly vigorous bulb and will spread quickly, providing even more colour with each passing year; it is good for naturalizing in grass. Team it with contrasting bright-coloured primulas and crocuses, Reticulata irises and hyacinths in pots or at the front of beds and borders.

Narcissus 'Jetfire'

○ ◐ ✗ ❖ EARLY SPRING
H 15–20cm (6–8in)

The rich orange trumpets of this little bulb set it apart from many similarly small daffodils. It also has swept-back petals that give it a certain elegance, despite its small size. 'Jetfire' looks good in large clumps in containers or borders. Plant it with crocuses, anemones and Reticulata irises or among heathers and foliage plants, including blue-leaved varieties such as the grass *Festuca glauca* 'Intense Blue'.

Narcissus 'Tête-à-tête'

○ ◐ ✗ ❖ EARLY SPRING
H 15cm (6in)

A very low-growing daffodil, this has flowers in two shades of deep yellow, the trumpets slightly darker than the petals. Each bulb produces a stem that may hold up to three flowers, giving even small clumps plenty of impact. For contrast grow it with deep-blue irises or rich-red primulas, or for a more subtle display choose primroses, which are pale yellow, or light pink double daisies.

Pericallis × *hybrida* 'Spring Glory'
Florist's cineraria

○ ◑ ✺ ❖ EARLY SPRING to EARLY SUMMER
H 20cm (8in)

The early-flowering cinerarias are tender perennials, and most are sold as house plants, but they can also be put in containers, including window boxes, in sheltered positions towards the end of spring. 'Spring Glory' is very floriferous, with flowers in single colours, including rich red, dark red, blue and pink, as well as bicolours, which are all these colours with white centres. Soften the plant's stiff appearance with trailing ivies.

Pericallis Senetti series
Senetti

○ ◑ ✺ ❖ EARLY SPRING to EARLY SUMMER
H 30–45cm (12–18in)

Senetti is a breeder's name given to a range of perennial cinerarias that, in the right conditions, will bloom indoors and then have a second flush of flowers outdoors. Very free-flowering, they are available in shades of blue, magenta and lavender blue, including bicolours. In containers underplant them with violas, trailing ivies, *Euonymus fortunei* varieties and other evergreens.

Primula Gold Laced Group

○ ◑ ❖ SPRING
H 10–15cm (4–6in)

This beautiful little perennial, with its yellow-edged, dark red-brown petals, used to be hard to find. Nowadays, you can buy it anywhere and there are red and pinkish versions, too. All deserve a special place in a container or at the front of a border where their elegance and fragrance can be appreciated.

Primula Polyanthus Group
Polyanthus

○ ◑ ❖ LATE WINTER to LATE SPRING
H 10–15cm (4–6in)

Polyanthus primulas produce a perennial rosette of tongue-shaped, dark green leaves and slender stalks that generally carry three or more flowers. The flower colours include yellow, red, dark blue, pink, white and a great number of shades in between. Most have a yellow centre. Grow primulas *en masse* at the front of flower beds or use them to brighten containers. They look good alone or with other plants, for example daffodils, crocuses and violas.

Primula Primlet series

○ ❖ LATE WINTER to EARLY SPRING
H 20cm (8in)

Who could resist these tiny, rosebud-like flowers? They come in a range of colours and most are lightly touched with paler or darker shades on the very edges of their petals. The delicate fragrance is strongest in the yellow shades. Plant them on their own in small containers or as part of a display with trailing ivy and small specimens of the conifer *Cupressus macrocarpa* 'Goldcrest'.

Ranunculus asiaticus Bloomingdale series
Persian buttercup

○ ❄ ⚒ ❖ SPRING to EARLY SUMMER
H 20–25cm (8–10in)

This tuberous plant has large, blowsy, double flowers in white, yellow, pink and red. A perennial, it needs to be dry in summer when it is dormant, so it is best grown in a container that can be put in a sheltered place. Grow it alone or with a contrasting foliage plant – for example, a small specimen of *Thuja occidentalis* 'Rheingold'.

Tulipa 'Mariette'
○ ✕ ❖ LATE SPRING
H 45–50cm (18–20in)

The Lily-flowered tulips have slender flowers opening wide above a slight waist that gives them a certain elegance. Grow them in tall containers or in borders. 'Mariette' has dark pink flowers that combine well with blue shades, such as forget-me-nots or a blue primula. Try it too with other Lily-flowered tulips – the contrasting 'West Point' (yellow) or complementary 'Ballade' (rose pink and white).

Tulipa 'Purissima'
○ ✕ ❖ MID-SPRING
H 35cm (14in)

The Fosteriana-type tulips have large, bowl-shaped flowers in mid-spring. 'Purissima' is a lovely example, with pure white flowers that look good with many spring flowers, including other tulips in almost any colour. This bulb can be planted in containers or *en masse* in borders. When combining different tulips, check plant height and flowering time, since these do vary quite considerably.

Tulipa 'Red Riding Hood'
○ ❖ EARLY SPRING
H 20cm (8in)

'Red Riding Hood' has scarlet, wide-opening flowers, each with a dark internal blotch. It is one of the low-growing Gregii tulips, which are ideal for slipping into small spaces, such as at the front of borders or in containers. The broad leaves, grey-green with darker markings, and comparatively large flowers look wonderful with small daffodils or foliage plants, such as the variegated ivy *Hedera helix* 'Glacier'.

Viola 'Frizzle Sizzle'
○ ◑ ❖ MID-SPRING to LATE SUMMER
H 23cm (9in)

This lovely showy pansy, with its heavily ruffled petals, doesn't pull any punches. For the best effect, group several plants, in a selection of shades, in a simple container. It comes in yellow, purple, mauve and white, each with the much-loved pansy 'face'. 'Fizzy' is similar, but slightly less frilly around the edges.

Viola 'Matrix Citrus Mix'
○ ◑ ❖ EARLY SPRING to EARLY SUMMER, WINTER
H 15–20cm (6–8in)

There are many different pansy varieties, but this has to be among the brightest of all, with small flowers in clean, sharp citrus colours that are quite shocking so early in the year. For the most effective display, grow it in groups in containers. Alternatively, combine it with a purple foliage plant – for example, *Ajuga reptans* 'Braunherz' – as a strong foil.

Viola 'Rebecca'
○ ◑ ❖ MID-SPRING to LATE SUMMER
H 10–15cm (4–6in)

There are so many violas available, but this one ought to make it into anyone's shopping basket, with its light fragrance and its pale creamy-white flowers tinged with purple. Plant 'Rebecca' on its own in a container or at the front of a border. Combine it with purple violets or with a small foliage plant: for example, *Euonymus fortunei* 'Emerald Gaiety' or the ivy *Hedera helix* 'Eva'.

Summer

Summer is the time for the most colourful displays, and this is also when we can best enjoy them outside. Bedding plants usually flower over a very long period, often into autumn, and many have a lovely scent. With interesting foliage plants too (*see* pages 79–83), there are plenty of ways to create pleasing colour and texture combinations.

Summer-flowering plants

All types of plants can be used for summer bedding: mainly annuals, but also bulbs, shrubs and tender perennials. If you buy young plants, remember to harden them off (*see* page 47) before planting out. There's something for every situation in the following pages.

Abutilon 'Bella' Flowering maple
○ ❁ ❖ MIDSUMMER to EARLY AUTUMN
H 40cm (16in)

With their large blooms in pastel shades of yellow, pink, orange and white, these perennial abutilons look as if they belong in the tropics. They're best in containers, placed where they can be viewed up close, such as beside a seating area. Underplant them with trailing foliage plants in silvery greens such as *Dichondra* 'Silver Falls' or *Helichrysum petiolare*.

Ageratum Floss flower
○ ❁ ❖ MIDSUMMER to MID- OR LATE AUTUMN
H 15–45cm (6–18in)

Ageratums are grown for their fluffy flowers, usually in blue, but they're also available in pink, white or bicolours: 'Tutti Booties' is a pastel mix; 'Timeless' is darker. They are all excellent for the front of borders, and taller types, such as 'Blue Horizon' (shown above), are good gap-fillers among perennials. They do well in containers, combined with plants that have an informal habit such as petunias and lobelias.

Amaranthus caudatus
Love-lies-bleeding
○ ❄ pH↑ ⚔ ❖ SUMMER to EARLY AUTUMN
H 0.9–1.5m (3–5ft)

This is a bushy, erect plant with fresh green leaves and long tassels of crimson-red flowers. It makes an excellent focal point and can be effective with other large bedding plants, such as cannas, rudbeckias or dahlias. It needs staking or a sheltered site. The tassels of 'Fat Spike' point upwards; those of *A.* 'Autumn Palette' are cream, pale orange and beige. Grow from seed.

Anchusa capensis 'Blue Angel'
Alkanet
○ ❄ ❖ SUMMER
H 20cm (8in)

Most anchusas have blue flowers and those of 'Blue Angel' are particularly dark and rich in colour. This is a compact form, whose soft outline makes it easy to combine with a variety of other plants in a mixed border or annual flower bed. Its colour makes it ideal for blending with pink flowers for a subtle harmony or yellow flowers for an eye-catching contrast. Grow from seed.

Angelonia Serena series
Summer snapdragon
○ ❁ ⚔ ❖ SUMMER
H 30–45cm (12–18in)

Available in white, purple, pink and lavender, these tender perennials have densely packed spikes of flowers, giving them great impact in the garden. Their soft colours make them suitable for planting in perennial borders as gap-fillers or with other annuals. They look good with blue-green foliage plants, such as the grass *Festuca glauca* 'Intense Blue', or could be planted with the similar snapdragons (*Antirrhinum*) for an interesting comparison of form.

Antirrhinum 'Appeal' Snapdragon
○ ❄ 人 ❖ SUMMER to EARLY AUTUMN
H 20cm (8in)

This is a compact, short-lived perennial and quite early to flower. It is sold as a mixture or in individual shades. If you want snapdragons in a pot, this is the type to go for; alternatively, plant it at the front of a flower bed, where it will look good with spreading annuals such as candytuft (*Iberis umbellata*) or sweet alyssum (*Lobularia maritima*). 'Liberty' is similar but much taller at 45cm (18in).

Argyranthemum frutescens
Marguerite
○ ❀ ❖ SUMMER
H 60–70cm (24–28in)

One of the most familiar of all bedding plants, marguerites (also known as *Chrysanthemum frutescens*) have pure white daisy flowers with yellow centres and grey-green leaves. At its best, this rounded, shrubby plant is smothered in blooms. Grow it as a centrepiece in a classy container, either alone or with a few trailing plants for company. It can be grown in flower beds, but will make less of an impact than when planted in pots.

Argyranthemum Madeira series
○ ❀ ❖ LATE SPRING to EARLY AUTUMN
H 30–45cm (12–18in)

Most argyranthemums make shrubby mounds of flowers throughout summer, and the Madeira series is no exception. Flowers range from white, through pale yellow, pink and burgundy – there's a colour for everyone. Some flowers are simple daisies, others are many-petalled pompons. Argyranthemums are best as the star performer in a container surrounded by plants that are lighter in form, including bacopas, lobelias, calibrachoas and *Helichrysum petiolare.*

Bacopa 'Snowflake'
○ ◑ ❀ ❖ SUMMER
H 8–10cm (3–4in)

Bacopas (also known as *Sutera*) have made a mark with their airy, trailing habit and tiny flowers. This one is a favourite, but all are perfect in a hanging basket or cascading down the sides of a pot, and look good with most other container plants. 'Lime Delight' has lime-green leaves and pale blue flowers; there are doubles in white, pink or blue. *Bacopa* 'Blutopia' has lovely lavender-blue flowers.

Begonia Devil's Delight series
○ ◑ ❀ pH ↓ ❖ SUMMER
H 15–20cm (6–8in)

This lovely collection of Semperflorens begonias can cope with either wet or dry summers. The foliage is shiny, dark bronze-red or green and the small, rounded flowers come in coral pink, rose pink, red and white. At their best along the front of borders, or *en masse* in island beds, *Begonia semperflorens* varieties also make good container plants, particularly for shallow pots. (*See also* page 64.)

Begonia Nonstop series
○ ◑ ❀ pH ↓ ❖ SUMMER
H 30cm (12in)

These Tuberhybrida begonias have big, rose-like, fully double flowers in a range of colours including red (as in 'Mocca Scarlet, shown above), white, yellow, peach and apricot. All Nonstop begonias look best as a feature plant in a pot, alone or with plants that have equally strong colours or forms. Try bidens, sanvitalia (both yellow) and foliage plants such as *Oxalis triangularis* or *Ipomoea* 'Black Tone'. (*See also* page 64.)

Above: *Begonia* 'Apricot Shades'. Right: *Begonia* 'Million Kisses Amour'.

Choosing begonias

The begonias used for bedding fall into two main groups: Tuberhybrida types, which grow from tubers, and Semperflorens types, which have fibrous roots. Tuberhybridas are known for their large, blowsy double flowers and big, pointed, oval leaves (height 30–38cm/12–15in). Sempflorens types are not as large (15–30cm/6–12in) and have rounded, succulent leaves and small but very colourful flowers. In addition, the tuberous begonias are sometimes divided into subgroups, including the Multiflora group, with many little, single to double flowers, and the Pendula group, with lax, trailing stems. All are available in a range of very bright colours, with green or bronze foliage.

Rex-type begonias, grown for their leaves in shades of green and purple with silvery markings, are increasingly used for containers, but are sensitive to cold temperatures and grow best above 21°C (70°F).

Growing begonias

Both the Semperflorens-type and Tuberhybrida-type begonias prefer well-drained soil that is humus-rich, fertile and slightly acid. They tolerate some shade and prefer not to be in full sun all day. Protect Tuberhybridas in containers from drying winds.

In the autumn, lift the tubers of Tuberhybridas and dry them off to store frost-free over winter. Plant them in pots in spring and they will reward you with many years of flowers. Watch out for vine weevil grubs, which can damage the stored tubers. The Multifloras tend to produce very small tubers and are best treated as annuals. Semperflorens types are usually discarded at the end of summer.

GOOD BEGONIA VARIETIES

Begonia 'Apricot Shades' (*see* above) – Pendula type with peachy flowers.

B. Devil's Delight series (*see* page 63) – weather-resistant Semperflorens type.

B. 'Dragon Wing' – Multiflora-type begonia with rounded, red flowers on pendant stems.

B. 'Gryphon' – A foliage begonia bred for sheltered outdoor sites.

B. 'Lotto' – A Semperflorens-type with large flowers in many colours.

B. Million Kisses series (*see* above) – Multiflora begonia with flowers in a range of colours.

B. Nonstop series (*see* page 63) – Tuberhybrida type with large flowers in a huge selection of colours.

Bidens ferulifolia
○ ❖ SUMMER to EARLY AUTUMN
H 20–30cm (8–12in)

The little, bright yellow flowers of bidens are borne on long stalks and surrounded by ferny foliage, making this a lovely, billowing plant for a hanging basket or the front of a window box. Grow it with more substantial plants such as busy lizzies (*Impatiens*) or petunias, or pair it with equally delicate ones, like bacopa, verbena or lobelia. It also looks good with ivy-leaved pelargoniums.

Brachyscome iberidifolia 'Blue Star' Swan river daisy
○ ❖ SUMMER
H 20–25cm (8–10in)

This spreading plant has violet-blue, star-shaped flowers above feathery, rich-green leaves. It is lovely in hanging baskets and other containers or, where the soil is well drained, it will succeed when planted in a border. Its soft form makes it suitable for filling gaps among low-growing perennials, and it is a complementary partner for a range of upright annuals, including ageratums and snapdragons (*Antirrhinum*).

Calceolaria 'Sunset' Slipper flower

○ ◑ ✿ pH ↓ ❖ SUMMER
H 15–20cm (6–8in)

The bright copper-orange, yellow or red flowers of this little plant make an eye-catching feature at the front of a border or in a container. Its shape is rather formal and, along with the rounded shape of the blooms, this can make it look a little unnatural. Reduce this effect by combining it with plants that have a spreading habit and smaller flowers, such as nemesia and diascia, and foliage plants such as grasses.

Calendula officinalis

Pot marigold
○ ◑ ✕ ❖ SUMMER to EARLY AUTUMN
H 12–24in (30–60cm)

A traditional cottage-garden annual, the pot marigold comes in orange, yellow and pink-yellow shades in double and single flowers. It has rich-green, aromatic foliage. Try it with blue flowers, such as love-in-a-mist (*Nigella*), or red ones, like salvias, or with everlasting flowers (*see* page 78). Good varieties include 'Indian Prince' (orange with brown markings, shown above) and 'Art Shades' (cream, soft orange, apricot). Grow from seed.

Calibrachoa Million bells

○ ◑ ✿ ❖ LATE SPRING to SUMMER
H 25–38cm (10–15in)

Calibrachoas produce masses of lovely, trumpet-shaped flowers, which resemble small petunias, on trailing stems. They are excellent in a hanging basket or container and look good with sanvitalias, bidens, verbenas, pelargoniums and lobelia. Million Bells series, with soft, mixed shades, is well known; other good varieties include Cabaret series (shown above), in strong, clean colours as well as pastels, and Can Can series, in apricot, terracotta and soft yellows.

Celosia argentea 'Dwarf Geisha'

○ ✿ ❖ SUMMER
H 20cm (8in)

This dwarf annual produces plume-like flowers in almost triangular heads above its foliage. The formal shape makes it ideal for traditional bedding, although it can be used among softer plants in informal borders. Plant the brighter colours – red and orange – with upright salvias for a complementary display; alternatively, choose lighter, gentler colours – cream, yellow and pink – and soften with grasses and billowing plants, such as isotomas and diascias.

Celosia argentea Kurume series

Cockscomb
○ ✿ ✕ ❖ SUMMER
H 90cm (3ft)

The flowers of this tall celosia are coiled into tight heads, hence its common name. Colours range from pink, scarlet and orange to bicoloured. Fascinating as it is, the flowers make it difficult to blend into borders: try it as a focal point or for architectural displays with other plants that have strong shapes, such as cannas, dahlias and love-lies-bleeding (*Amaranthus caudatus*). Grow from seed.

Centaurea cyanus 'Black Ball'

○ pH ↑ ✕ ❖ SUMMER to EARLY AUTUMN
H 90cm (3ft)

With its fluffy, rounded flowerheads in dark maroon-red, this is a lovely version of the blue wild cornflower. Both are ideal for an informal border and for filling gaps among perennials. They look excellent contrasting with orange pot marigolds (*Calendula*) or with plants in complementary shades, such as dark blue love-in-a-mist (*Nigella*) or salvias. Their silver-green foliage combines well with the feathery leaves of *Senecio cineraria* 'Silver Dust'. Grow from seed.

Clarkia elegans

○ ◐ ❄ pH↓ ✄ ❖ MIDSUMMER to EARLY AUTUMN
H 60–90cm (2–3ft)

A tall, upright annual with flowers in various shades of pink to dark purple, this is a traditional cottage-garden favourite. It is easy to place among taller perennials and its height makes it useful for filling gaps towards the back of flower beds. Clarkias dislike transplanting, so are best sown *in situ* in spring or autumn (protect with a cloche). 'Passion for Purple' is a shorter variety, with deeply cut, purple flowers.

Cleome spinosa
'Colour Fountain' Spider flower

○ ❁ ❖ SUMMER to AUTUMN
H 1.2–1.5m (4–5ft)

The thick, spiny stems of the spider flower carry delicate spirals of flowers in shades of pink, white and magenta. Its stiff habit and rather coarse leaves make it best placed among softer shapes, such as cosmos, towards the back of borders where it will flower well into autumn without needing any staking. The flowers are replaced by horizontal seedpods, which are quite attractive too.

Consolida ajacis 'Moody Blues'
Larkspur

○ ◐ ✄ ❖ SUMMER
H 90cm (3ft)

Closely related to the very similar-looking perennial delphiniums, the annual larkspurs often have fewer flowers per spike, which gives them a wispy elegance. 'Moody Blues' is a lovely mix of blues, whites and near-grey. It combines well with poppies (*Papaver*), cornflowers (*Centaurea*) and gypsophila. Short varieties, such as 'Dwarf Rocket' (to 50cm/20in), are not as elegant but their stockiness allows them to be put in more exposed sites. Grow from seed.

Cosmos bipinnatus

○ ❁ ✄ ❖ SUMMER to AUTUMN
H 1.2m (4ft)

Most cosmos (sometimes known as *Cosmea*) have bright green, feathery foliage, making them easy to place among perennials in borders and useful for softening the stiff appearance of some upright annuals. They look good with dahlias and grasses, too. 'Purity' (shown above) has white blooms, while 'Sensation Mixed' comes in shades of white and pink to rich magenta.

Dahlia Gallery series

○ ❁ ✄ ❖ MIDSUMMER to AUTUMN
H 40cm (16in)

Dahlias are tender perennials and this collection is sold as flowering plants for summer bedding. They are ideal for filling gaps in flower beds, either among other temporary plants such as cosmos, ageratums and zinnias, or with mid- and late-summer flowering perennials, for example rudbeckias and salvias. Good varieties include 'Art Nouveau' (cerise, shown above), 'Art Deco' (peachy orange), 'Pablo' (creamy-yellow, orange flares) and 'Renoir' (candy pink).

Dianthus barbatus
'Festival Mixed' Sweet william

○ pH↑ ✄ ❖ LATE SPRING to EARLY SUMMER
H 60cm (2ft)

Each stem of a sweet william produces a rounded bunch of wonderfully scented flowers, and this mixture comes in a range of white, pink and rose shades, including some with petals banded or edged in white. It is a short-lived perennial, usually grown as a biennial, and is often teamed with the beautiful soft-blue flowers and feathery foliage of love-in-a-mist (*Nigella*).

Diascia
○ ❄ ❖ SUMMER to AUTUMN
H 25–30cm (10–12in)

There are numerous diascias in a range of colours, from bright pink and orange-red to soft pastels and bicolours. You can get trailing varieties for hanging baskets and tubs, or more upright types for edging beds. Wink series diascias are upright and available in pinks, orange (above) and white; Whisper series consists of apricot, rich-red and pastel orange flowers with a trailing habit.

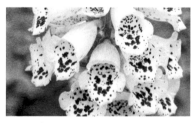

Digitalis purpurea Foxglove
○ ◑ ❖ LATE SPRING to EARLY SUMMER
H 0.3–2m (1–6ft)

The lovely biennial foxglove smooths the transition between spring and summer, providing height, colour and elegance. For the front or middle of a border, choose dwarf varieties, such as 'Carillion' (creamy white, H 30cm/12in) or 'Foxy' (white, cream, pink or red, with pinkish-maroon spots, H 90cm/3ft, shown above). However, full-height versions are particularly striking; they look splendid planted under trees and go well with most other late-spring flowers. Foxgloves will grow in pots but are much better in the soil.

Eschscholzia californica
California poppy
○ ❄ ❖ SUMMER to EARLY AUTUMN
H 30cm (12in)

Characterized by bright orange flowers and blue-green, ferny foliage, the California poppy is wonderful *en masse* on dry banks and in gravel. The flowers close in gloomy weather. Combine it with similarly coloured marigolds or blue flowers such as *Salvia farinacea* 'Victoria'. For a sophisticated display, choose the variety 'Carmine King' (pink with a pale centre). Grow from seed.

Euryops pectinatus
○ ❄ ❖ SUMMER to MID-AUTUMN
H 60cm (2ft)

A softly shrubby plant, this produces pure yellow daisy flowers on long, wiry stalks above divided, greyish leaves. In ideal conditions it can become quite substantial and is best appreciated in a large container or as a feature plant in a mixed border. It will survive over winter if brought under cover and will continue flowering in good light and warmth.

Felicia amelloides 'Variegata'
Blue daisy
○ ❄ ❖ SUMMER to AUTUMN
H 30–35cm (12–14in)

This little shrubby plant is valued for its bright blue daisy flowers carried on slender stems above white-variegated, oval leaves: a delightful combination, especially in a terracotta pot. It prefers good drainage, so is best planted in a container or hanging basket or in a very dry spot in the garden. Grow it with pelargoniums or a foliage plant, such as *Alternanthera dentata*.

Fuchsia 'Genii'
○ ◑ ❄ ❖ SUMMER to AUTUMN
H 35–75cm (14–30in)

The lime-green leaves of 'Genii' are particularly effective in a shady spot and make a lovely foil for the red-and-violet flowers. It is a shrub with an upright habit, so make it a feature under a tree or plant it in a container destined for a shady corner. Begonias, pansies and busy lizzies (*Impatiens*), in yellow, orange or dark pink, make good companions.

Fuchsia 'Lena'
○ ◑ ❄ ❖ SUMMER to AUTUMN
H 30–45cm (12–18in)

This shrub has a semi-pendent habit, making it an ideal choice for the edge of a container or hanging basket. It has abundant rounded, pink-white and magenta flowers and looks good on its own or with pink or purple petunias or similarly richly coloured verbena or lobelia. Red or pink begonias also look good with it, especially the trailing types with smallish flowers.

Gaillardia pulchella
Blanket flower
○ ✕ ❖ SUMMER to AUTUMN
H 30–45cm (12–18in)

A particularly flamboyant annual, this has large, daisy heads of flowers in red and yellow. 'Razzle Dazzle' has double flowers that look like fluffy pompons in yellow, cream, orange, rich burgundy-red and bicolours. 'Red Plume' (shown above) has double, deep-red flowers. 'Arizona' has single, red flowers edged yellow. Grow big clumps in borders with dahlias and similarly bright flowers, or use one as a feature plant in a container.

Gazania Daybreak series
○ ❀ ❖ SUMMER
H 25cm (10in)

Gazanias are low-growing perennials with dark green leaves that are silvery-hairy underneath. Their flowers, a bit like small sunflowers, open only on sunny days. 'Tiger Stripe' (above) has yellow, orange or white petals with a fairly wide, red stripe along the centre. 'Bronze' is orange with a darker centre. Grow them at the front of borders or in pots and window boxes.

Gladiolus
○ ❀ ✕ ❖ SUMMER
H to 1.5m (5ft) or more

It is well worth planting gladiolus corms in late spring, since they will reward you with tall spikes of large, colourful flowers for several weeks over summer. They have pale green, sword-shaped leaves and flowers in a wide range of colours, including rich red ('Black Jack', shown above), yellow ('Jester'), green with red edges ('Laguna') and violet-blue ('Blue Isle'). Grow them in borders with dahlias, love-lies-bleeding (*Amaranthus cordatus*), poppies (*Papaver*) and grasses.

Gypsophila elegans
'Covent Garden' Baby's breath
○ pH↑ ✕ ❖ SUMMER
H 60cm (2ft)

A traditional cottage-garden favourite, this little annual has grey-green leaves at the base of spindly stems covered with masses of tiny, white flowers. Sow seed directly into the soil among almost any other annuals to soften their form and create a gentle, fuzzy whiteness. It looks particularly good with poppies (*Papaver*) and cornflowers (*Centaurea*), but also makes an interesting partner for pot marigolds (*Calendula*).

Helianthus annuus Sunflower
○ pH↑ ✕ ❖ MIDSUMMER to EARLY AUTUMN
H to 4m (13ft) or more

If you can't fit the tallest sunflowers in your garden, don't despair: they now come in almost any size. In fact, shorter types often have many flowers per stem. Try 'Moulin Rouge' (shown above, H to 2m/6ft), 'Pastiche' (orange and yellow shades, H to 1.5m/5ft) or 'Teddy Bear' (fluffy, yellow flowers, H 60cm/2ft). Grow them in borders among other tall or medium-sized annuals. Most are easy to grow from seed.

Heliotropium arborescens
'Marine' Cherry pie, Heliotrope
○ ❁ ❖ SUMMER to EARLY AUTUMN
H 45cm (18in)

The lovely, deep violet-blue flowers of
this shrubby perennial have a heady
scent, so position this little plant where
you can have a good sniff as you pass
by. It makes an excellent edging to
flower beds or will do well in a container.
The leaves are rich dark green. The plant
has quite a stiff habit, which can be
disguised by combining it with pansies,
gypsophila or love-in-a-mist (Nigella).

Iberis umbellata Candytuft
○ pH↑ ❖ MID-SPRING to SUMMER
H 15–30cm (6–12in)

A traditional cottage-garden favourite,
candytuft has scented, rounded
flowerheads in shades of white, pink,
magenta and lilac above narrow leaves.
It is suitable for growing at the edges of
borders and in containers. 'Flash Mixed'
(shown above) is particularly richly
coloured. Combine it with foliage plants
such as Senecio cineraria 'Silver Dust' and
hare's tail grass (Lagurus ovatus).

Impatiens (Busy lizzie)

Impatiens Fiesta series produces double
blooms in shades of red, pink and purple.

GOOD BUSY LIZZIE VARIETIES

Impatiens Accent series – vivid colours
including some flowers with
white crosses.

I. 'Fanfare' (see page 70) – semi-
trailing New Guinea hybrid.

I. Fiesta series (see left) – masses of
double flowers in pinks, reds and
purples.

I. 'Masquerade' (see below) – lipstick-
red flowers above eye-catching,
glossy, yellow-variegated foliage.

I. Sunpatiens series – flowers can
withstand dry and wet conditions;
'Volcano' is lava red.

Choosing busy lizzies

Impatiens is a large group of plants
with succulent foliage and a bushy,
sometimes shrubby habit. There are
two main types, both with many
variations: Impatiens walleriana
hybrids and Impatiens New Guinea
hybrids. You are unlikely to see
'walleriana' types referred to as such,
since the plants that are cultivated
today have developed well beyond
their original parentage. They do
share some similarities, however, such
as pale green, slightly toothed leaves
and a small, shrub-like habit. They are
available in small to medium sizes,
varying in height from 15 to 30cm
(6 to 12in). New Guinea hybrids (see
page 70) are bigger (up to 40cm/16in
or more), with larger, generally more
pointed leaves in richer colours.

Growing busy lizzies

All busy lizzies like well-drained soil
that contains plenty of humus and is
reasonably fertile. They tolerate some
sun but prefer partial shade. In pots
they need regular watering; the New

Guinea types are particularly prone to
wilting when short of water, but soon
recover once watered. New Guinea
hybrids can be brought indoors to a
light spot in autumn and will flower
until late autumn. Water them
moderately and they will survive
winter, too.

Busy lizzies are easy to propagate
from cuttings. Take these in spring or
early summer, just below a leaf joint
(see page 48).

Impatiens downy mildew is a
fungal disease that can devastate busy
lizzies. Their leaves turn yellow and
drop off. Affected plants don't recover
and should be destroyed. Fortunately,
the disease affects only busy lizzies.

Impatiens 'Masquerade' has yellow-
variegated leaves and single, red flowers.

Impatiens New Guinea hybrids
Busy lizzie

○ ◑ ✿ ❖ SUMMER to AUTUMN

H 35–40cm (14–16in)

The perennial New Guinea impatiens are almost like small shrubs, with attractive, rich-green or purple-tinted foliage and large, brightly coloured flowers. Grow them in pots either on their own or with begonias and fuchsias. 'Celerio' (shown above) has bright pink, double flowers and dark green leaves with yellow central flashes, while 'Strike' has yellow-variegated foliage. (*See also* page 69.)

Lavatera trimestris Mallow

○ ✄ ❖ SUMMER

H 90–120cm (3–4ft)

The annual mallows are tall, bushy plants, with lobed, green leaves and big, wide-open flowers, a bit like hibiscus. The petals have a satiny appearance. 'Mont Blanc' (shown above) is ice white; 'Silver Cup' has rose-pink flowers with darker veins. Grow them in borders with gypsophila, cornflowers (*Centaurea*), opium poppies (*Papaver somniferum*), love-lies-bleeding (*Amaranthus cordatus*), grasses and castor-oil plant (*Ricinus communis*). Raise from seed.

Linaria maroccana 'Northern Lights'

○ ❖ SUMMER

H 30–60cm (12–24in)

This lovely plant deserves to be more widely grown. It has rich-green leaves on wiry stems and delicate, snapdragon-like flowers in yellow, rich pink, pale pink, purple and white. It is attractive planted *en masse* at the front of a border and makes a good gap-filler in perennial beds. Grow it with California poppies (*Eschscholzia californica*), field poppies (*Papaver rhoeas*) and cornflowers (*Centaurea*) as a nod to a wildflower meadow. Grow from seed.

Isotoma axillaris

○ ✿ ❖ SUMMER

H 10–30cm (4–12in)

This plant (sometimes called *Laurentia* or *Solenopsis*) has slender, lobed leaves and properly star-shaped flowers. The flowers are slightly scented. They are usually blue (as in 'Blue Star', shown above), but other colours may be found, such as a range of pink, blue and white ('Avante-Garde'). Isotomas look wonderful on their own in a container, revealing their soft, evenly rounded shape, but are also good with trailing annuals, such as petunias and bacopa.

Lilium Lily

○ ◑ ✄ ❖ SUMMER

H 0.3–3m (1–10ft)

Lilies come in a huge range of sizes and shades. Some are short, brightly coloured and faintly scented; others are very tall and highly perfumed. However, there is little to better old-fashioned, mid-height (H 0.9–1.5m/3–5ft), strongly scented varieties like 'African Queen' (rich yellow), 'Casablanca' (white) and 'Star Gazer' (dark pink, shown above). Plant the bulbs in pots to plunge into gaps in borders or to place near seats.

Lobelia erinus (compact)

○ ◑ ✿ ❖ SUMMER to AUTUMN

H 10–15cm (4–6in)

Most people think of lobelia as trailing (*see* opposite), but there are compact varieties that do well at the front of borders and edging paths as well as in containers. The best include 'Cambridge Blue' (pale blue), 'Crystal Palace' (dark blue), 'Mrs Clibran' (dark blue with white eyes) and 'Rosamund' (cerise, shown above). They make an excellent contrast to bright-flowered busy lizzies (*Impatiens*), pelargoniums and nicotianas.

Lobelia erinus (trailing)
◯ ◐ ❀ ❖ SUMMER to AUTUMN
H 15cm (6in)

Until the advent of modern trailing varieties of many other annuals, lobelias were more or less the only plant that went around the edge of containers and hanging baskets. They still hold their own in this department and look excellent with brilliant red pelargoniums and pink fuchsias. Cascade series is available in several shades of blue (such as lavender, shown above) and white, while Regatta series, also available in blue and white, is early flowering.

Lupinus Gallery series Lupin
◯ ◐ pH↓ ❖ LATE SPRING to MIDSUMMER
H 50–60cm (20–24in)

Lupins are usually grown as perennials, but in some areas they are short-lived and are best as annuals. They have attractive leaves and tall spires of peppery-scented flowers. Gallery series is available in pink, red, white, yellow, blue (shown above) and bicolours. It is ideal midway into borders, filling gaps or growing with other tallish plants like foxgloves (*Digitalis*) and cannas.

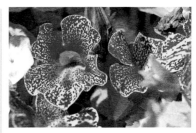

Mimulus Magic series
Monkey flower
◯ ◐ ❖ SUMMER
H 15–20cm (6–8in)

This little plant produces surprisingly large, open-faced flowers in a range of bright colours including orange, yellow, red and bicolours, with spots, stipples ('Yellow Flame', shown above) and pastel shading. They can be difficult to place among other garden plants because of their strong shapes, but look good with marigolds (*Tagetes*) and foliage plants. They also brighten a shady corner.

Lobularia maritima Sweet alyssum
◯ ❖ SUMMER
H 8–30cm (3–12in)

The tiny individual flowers of sweet alyssum (sometimes known as *Alyssum maritimum*) are clustered into rounded heads above the leaves. Put these low-growing plants beside paths and seating areas, where you can benefit from their lovely scent, or grow them in pots with other traditional bedding such as pelargoniums, busy lizzies and begonias. Good varieties include 'Clear Crystal' (white, shown above) and 'Easter Bonnet' (red, purple, white and pink).

Matthiola incana Stock
◯ pH↑ ⚒ ❖ LATE SPRING to MIDSUMMER
H to 30cm (12in) or more

Stocks are grown for their scented flowers carried on tall stems above grey-green foliage. They come in a range of colours, including pale and dark pink, lilac and white. Group them together and soften their strong outlines with gypsophila, field poppies (*Papaver rhoeas*) or love-in-a-mist (*Nigella*). Good varieties include: 'Giant Perfection' (shown above, H 45cm/18in), 'Ten Week Mixed' (H 30cm/12in) and 'Cinderella Mixed' (H 20–30cm/8–12in).

Molucella laevis Bells of Ireland
◯ ⚒ ❖ LATE SUMMER
H 60–75cm (24–30in)

Bells of Ireland has tall spikes of fragrant flowers, each surrounded by a large, bright green calyx, which overwhelms the tiny flower within; the pale green leaves have toothed edges. This is a strongly architectural plant that looks good with softer shapes, such as grasses, and with bright flowers, including opium poppies (*Papaver somniferum*), taller marigolds (*Tagetes*), lupins and nicotianas. Grow from seed.

Nemesia Aromatica series
○ ◑ ❀ pH↓ ❖ SUMMER
H 30–35cm (12–14in)

Aromatica is a collection of nemesias picked for their rich and appealing colours and strong, sweet fragrance. They have an upright habit and are ideal for pots; they thrive in flower beds, too. Their strong colours combine well with yellow and orange, such as low-growing Signet or French marigolds (*Tagetes*). They can also hold their own among bright busy lizzies (*Impatiens*).

Nemophila menziesii
Baby blue eyes
○ ◑ ❖ SUMMER
H 15–20cm (6–8in)

This is a charming little plant that goes well around the edges of containers as well as along paths, beside steps and in paving cracks. It has a spreading habit with small, toothed, soft grey-green leaves and rounded, bright blue flowers on long stalks. Grow it with *Dianthus chinensis*, violas, diascias and nemesias. 'Penny Black' has nearly black flowers with white edges. Grow from seed.

Nigella damascena Love-in-a-mist
○ ❖ SUMMER
H 20cm (18in)

Everyone loves this plant for its feathery foliage and pale blue flowers with their pointed petals and filigree ruffs. Pretty, rounded seedheads form as the flowers fade. Its unassuming nature allows it to partner a wide range of plants, from cornflowers (*Centaurea*) to nicotianas, isotoma, lilies and marigolds (*Tagetes*). Good varieties include 'Miss Jekyll' (sky blue, shown above) and 'Persian Jewels' (blue, pink and white). Grow from seed.

Nemesia 'Berries and Cream'
○ ◑ ❀ pH↓ ❖ SUMMER
H 35cm (14in)

One of many superb nemesias, 'Berries and Cream' stands out for its lovely soft-pink and rich-lilac colouring and its sweet perfume. It is a wonderful plant for a hanging basket, pot or window box and combines well with pastel busy lizzies (*Impatiens*), argyranthemums, lobelia and pale fuchsias. 'Amelie' is pinky lilac and also very fragrant.

Nicotiana 'Lime Green'
Tobacco plant
○ ◑ ❀ ❖ SUMMER to EARLY AUTUMN
H 60cm (24in)

'Lime Green' is one of the most desirable of all bedding nicotianas for its light green flowers, which look good with pale busy lizzies (*Impatiens*), cornflowers (*Centaurea*) and love-in-a-mist (*Nigella*) as well as with stronger colours, such as pink cosmos and red pelargoniums. Or try it with a purple foliage plant, like alternanthera or *Strobilanthes dyeriana*.

Osteospermum Serenity series
African daisy
○ ❀ ❖ LATE SPRING to AUTUMN
H 25–35cm (10–14in)

This collection of African daisies has been selected for its long season of flowering and compact, bushy plants, as well as its lovely flower colours, which include pink (shown above), dark purple, yellow ('Lemonade') and pink fading to cream ('Sunset'). Grow African daisies in a sheltered spot at the front of a border or in containers with foliage plants such as *Helichrysum petiolare*.

Papaver rhoeas Field poppy
○ ❖ SUMMER
H to 90cm (3ft)

Field poppies are traditional cottage-garden plants and are very easy to slip into gaps in perennial borders or to grow with a range of other annuals, both old-fashioned and more modern. Shirley (shown above) is a pretty, well-established range of single, semi-double and double flowers in shades of yellow, pink, orange and red. 'Mother of Pearl' has flowers in soft pinks, lilac and almost grey. Grow from seed.

Papaver somniferum 'Paeony Flowered' Opium poppy
○ ❖ SUMMER
H 90–120cm (3–4ft)

Opium poppies are upright with deeply lobed, blue-green leaves and large, bowl-shaped flowers in pink, purple, red or white. They combine well with other annuals and perennials, and look good with cosmos, clarkia and blue salvias. 'Paeony Flowered' has large, frilly, double flowers in various pink shades, red or white. Distinctive pepper-pot seedheads follow the flowers. Grow from seed.

Pelargonium

Above: *Pelargonium* 'Fireworks Red-White'.
Above right: *Pelargonium* 'Angeleyes Orange'.
Right: Ivy-leaved *Pelargonium* 'L'Elégante'.

Choosing pelargoniums

Often (but incorrectly) known as geraniums, pelargoniums are a very varied bunch of plants. Most are grown for their bright flowers, but there are some that are also grown for their heavily scented or attractively variegated foliage (*see* page 82).

The two pelargoniums most commonly used for bedding are defined by their foliage: zonal and ivy-leaved. Those developed from regal types are also gaining favour. Zonals have stiff, upright stems and soft, usually rounded, green leaves, often with darker flushes or mottling, and a distinctive smell. Ivy-leaved are usually trailing, with pointed, lobed leaves that are shiny, stiff and fleshy, and have no fragrance. Regals are popular house plants with rich-green, deeply divided leaves.

Pelargonium flowers are single, semi-double or double, some like tiny rosebuds, and come in reds, pinks, mauve, salmon, white and bicolours.

Growing pelargoniums

All pelargoniums prefer well-drained, alkaline soil and a sunny position, although zonal types tolerate some shade. Most are reasonably drought-tolerant and all do very well in containers. If you live in a wet area, choose single-flowered varieties, since frequent rain encourages the petals of doubles to stick together and rot. Pelargoniums cannot survive frost, but you can bring them indoors over winter. With enough warmth and light they will continue to flower. Otherwise, reduce watering and cut them back by about one third. Repot them in late winter or early spring for another year of colour. Take cuttings to increase your stock (*see* page 48).

GOOD PELARGONIUM VARIETIES

Pelargonium 'Angeleyes Orange' (*see* above) – regal, with small, orange-pink flowers with deeper centres.

P. Fireworks series (*see* above) – zonal, neat, upright habit; pointed petals.

P. 'Lady Plymouth' (*see* page 82 – scented-leaved, with small flowers.

P. 'L'Elégante' (*see* above) – ivy-leaved, white variegations; dainty, single, white flowers with crimson markings.

P. 'Mrs Pollock' – zonal, yellow-edged, green-and-red leaves; red flowers.

P. 'Vancouver Centennial' (*see* page 82) – zonal, green leaves heavily flushed maroon; pale red flowers.

Pelargonium Black Velvet series
◯ ◗ ✿ pH ↑ ❖ SUMMER to AUTUMN
H 30cm (12in)

In this group of zonal pelargoniums, dark chocolate-brown leaves make a stunning backdrop for the brightly coloured, semi-double flowerheads. Each leaf has a fine green edge. 'Rose' (shown above) has pale pink flowers with white flashes. Other colours include salmon, scarlet, pink and coral. Grow them in containers with pale green or silver foliage plants, such as helichrysum. (*See also* page 73.)

Penstemon 'Laura'
◯ ◗ ❖ SUMMER to AUTUMN
H 70cm (28in)

Penstemons are occasionally grown as perennials, but some are rather tender and often short-lived. They have tall spikes of tubular flowers in a range of different colours, including bicolours such as 'Laura' (shown above), and are ideal for gap-filling in perennial borders, where they look comfortable among perennial geraniums, salvias and grasses. Also, try combining them with annuals such as love-in-a-mist (*Nigella*) and opium poppies (*Papaver somniferum*).

Petunia Frenzy Mixed selection
◯ ◗ ✿ ❖ SUMMER to EARLY AUTUMN
H 30cm (12in)

This selection of petunias is popular for its extremely wide range of colours – there are over 20, including flowers with white stripes or heavy, dark veining and many soft pastel shades as well as strong primary ones. The plants are compact but trail well, and they are good in all types of containers with other annuals.

Petunia Surfinia series
◯ ◗ ✿ ❖ SUMMER to EARLY AUTUMN
H 30–90cm (12–36in)

Surfinia petunias have large flowers on bushy, many-branched, long-trailing plants. More weather-resistant than the older varieties, their flowers can withstand some rain. They are perfect for hanging baskets and window boxes, and can be combined with many other plants including bidens, fuchsias, sanvitalias, lobelia and pelargoniums. 'Tidal Wave' (shown above) is a good mixture of bright colours.

Petunia Tumbelina series
◯ ◗ ✿ ❖ SUMMER to EARLY AUTUMN
H 45cm (18in)

Tumbelina petunias have peony-like, ruffled, double flowers in lilac ('Priscilla', shown above), white, pink, yellow-green and deep red, with some bicolours and heavy veining. The blooms have been bred to withstand rain and some are highly fragrant. They look impressive in hanging baskets and window boxes with pelargoniums, verbenas and lobelia. For a more refined summer display, combine petunias with foliage plants.

Phlox drummondii 'Phlox of Sheep'
◯ ❖ SUMMER
H 30cm (12in)

This is a witty name for a lovely annual that has rounded flowers in creamy yellow, pink and salmon pink. They are carried in rounded heads at the top of tallish stems. The soft colour mix makes the plants suitable for slipping into gaps in perennial borders or adding to annual schemes. Try them with field poppies (*Papaver rhoeas*), love-in-a-mist (*Nigella*), nicotianas, molucellas and salvias.

Ptilotus exaltatus 'Joey'
○ ❖ SUMMER
H 30–35cm (12–14in)

Ptilotus has rosettes of thick, blue-green leaves with wavy edges. Its pink flowers are carried in pointed spikes and are surrounded by fine, white hairs, giving it a bottlebrush-like appearance. Ptilotus dislikes wet conditions, so it's best to grow it in a raised bed, in a gap on a wall or in a container. Combine it with other drought-tolerant plants such as osteospermums and gazanias.

Rudbeckia hirta
○ ❖ SUMMER to EARLY AUTUMN
H 30–90cm (12–36in)

Rudbeckias are biennials with large, daisy-like flowers in shades of orange, yellow, marmalade, deep red and nearly brown, all with pronounced, usually dark centres. 'Cherokee Sunset' (shown above) has double flowers in rich bronze shades. Use it to fill gaps in perennial borders or combine it with gaillardias, salvias, dahlias and shorter sunflowers (*Helianthus*). 'Rustic Dwarfs Mixed' has single flowers in similar colours.

Salpiglossis sinuata 'Royale Mixed'
○ ◐ ✿ ⚔ ❖ SUMMER to AUTUMN
H 60cm (24in)

Given a good, warm summer, this somewhat sprawling plant will produce quantities of large, trumpet-shaped flowers in deep, rich, exotic colours with dark veining in their yellowing throats. Since it needs a sheltered spot, it is best in a container on a sunny patio, where it looks wonderful with other flamboyant flowers including argyranthemums, pelargoniums and schizanthus.

Salvia farinacea 'Victoria'
○ ◐ ✿ ❖ SUMMER to LATE AUTUMN
H 60cm (24in)

This is a compact plant with plenty of low branches, each producing a spike of small, deep-blue flowers. It also has dense, rich-green foliage, giving it plenty of solidity right down to the ground. Grow it at the front of borders or as a gap-filler among perennials. 'Seascape', which is shorter (H 35–40cm/14–16in), has a mixture of blue and silver flowers.

Salvia guaranitica 'Black and Blue'
○ ◐ ✿ ❖ LATE SUMMER to LATE AUTUMN
H to 2m (6ft) or more

One of the more refined salvias, 'Black and Blue' has rough, oval leaves and tall, stiff stems topped with slender spikes of rich-blue flowers opening from dark blue buds. The effect is attractive and elegant. An excellent plant for cooling a hot border, it would go well with purple pennisetums and taller rudbeckias, perhaps towering behind bedding dahlias.

Salvia viridis Clary
○ ◐ ⚔ ❖ SUMMER to AUTUMN
H 40–45cm (16–18in)

Clary is an old-fashioned garden annual with spikes of tiny flowers, each surrounded by large, papery bracts in white, pink or deep purple-blue. It looks good growing *en masse* at the edge of borders and also creates an excellent disguise for the bare legs of sweet peas (*Lathyrus*). The flowers can be dried. Grow from seed.

Sanvitalia procumbens

○ ❀ ❖ SUMMER to EARLY AUTUMN

H 20cm (8in)

This is a wide-spreading, mat-forming plant that produces small, rich-green leaves and bright yellow flowers like tiny sunflowers – they are only 2cm (¾in) across. It flowers very generously, creating a bright splash of sunshine at the front of a window box and around the edge of a container. Try combining it with other yellow flowers, such as calibrachoas or argyranthemums, as well as blues and reds.

Schizanthus pinnatus
'Hit Parade' Poor man's orchid

○ ❀ ✗ ❖ SPRING to AUTUMN

H to 30cm (12in)

Rather a rarity in gardens, schizanthus deserves to be more widely grown for its tubular flowers with their wide-spreading, often slightly lobed petals. The flower colours include red, mauve, pink and white with paler, heavily marked throats. It is best in a sheltered spot, so grow it in containers on a patio with other bright flowers, such as petunias and pelargoniums.

Tagetes (Marigold)

Left: *Tagetes* 'Bonanza Mix'. Above: *Tagetes* 'Taishan Orange'.

Choosing marigolds

Marigolds (*Tagetes*) are refreshingly simple plants of the what-you-see-is-what-you-get variety. They have no airs and graces and are available only in shades of yellow, orange and red, usually flowering from late spring to early autumn. The other noticeable thing about them is their pungent aroma.

Their names can be confusing. African marigolds (*T. erecta*), also known as American marigolds, are upright and have large heads of pompon flowers. French marigolds (*T. patula*), which are also usually upright but smaller, may have single or double flowers, often with some red-brown colouring. Signet marigolds (*T. tenuifolia*), sometimes also known as French marigolds, often have a relaxed habit and single flowers. Within these groups there are many variations, so it's best to check the label for a description.

The African marigolds are ideal for formal bedding, while the others are more suitable for the edge of a mixed border. All are suitable for containers.

GOOD MARIGOLD VARIETIES

Tagetes Bonanza series (*see above*) – French with double flowers in red, orange and yellow. H 30cm (12in).

T. Disco series – French with single flowers in yellow, gold-red, gold with red markings and orange. H to 25cm (8in).

T. 'Durango Red' – French with yellow-edged, scarlet-red flowers. H to 25cm (10in).

T. 'French Vanilla' – African with creamy-white flowers. H 38cm (15in).

T. Gem series (*see* opposite) – Signet in a range of bold colours.

T. 'Starfire' – Signet in orange, yellow, red and bicolours. H 20cm (8in).

T. Taishan series (*see above*) – African with flowers in yellow, orange and gold. H 30cm (12in).

Growing marigolds

All marigolds like well-drained soil in a sunny situation, which is in any case where their bright flowers look best. The larger, more double, pompon flowerheads can suffer in wet weather, although breeding work is combating this. Marigolds are half-hardy and some can suffer in cold weather, when their foliage turns purple. They are easy to raise from seed, but many varieties are available as growing plants too.

Tagetes Gem series
○ ❀ ❖ LATE SPRING to EARLY AUTUMN
H 20–23cm (8–9in)

This is a collection of Signet marigolds with single flowers in yellow ('Lemon Gem', shown above), orange with a yellow edge ('Paprika Gem') and deep orange ('Tangerine Gem'). Like all Signet marigolds, they are perfect for growing among other flowering annuals, looking particularly good with argyranthemums and zinnias, or for filling in gaps towards the front of perennial borders.

Torenia 'Clown Mixed'
Wishbone flower
◐ ❀ ❖ SUMMER
H 20–25cm (8–10in)

Torenias are pretty, neat little plants with rich-green, serrated leaves and comparatively big flowers with flaring petals. They make an exotic-looking addition to a sheltered patio. Grow them in pots on their own or with trailing foliage plants such as dicondra or *Glechoma hederacea* 'Variegata'. *Torenia* 'Clown Mixed' has petals in yellow, purple and pink with white throats.

Viola 'Friolina Cascadiz'
○ ◐ ❖ SPRING to AUTUMN
H 1m (40in)

If you like delicate viola flowers and hanging baskets, this biennial gives you the chance to put them together. It has very long, trailing stems covered with fragrant flowers in gold, purple-blue, blue and gold, creamy pink and pastel orange. Try it with other plants or grow several in a hanging basket for a fabulous display. 'Avalanche' is shorter (23cm/9in) with flowers in soft colours, including pink, violet and yellow.

Tithonia rotundifolia 'Torch'
Mexican sunflower
○ ❀ ❖ LATE SUMMER to AUTUMN
H 0.3–2m (1–6ft)

A good plant for a sheltered hot summer border, *Tithonia rotundifolia* can grow very tall, given warm, dry conditions. 'Torch' has large flowers in shades of red and orange, and its leaves are pointed and often lobed. Tithonia combines well with tall orange or red dahlias as well as cannas and rudbeckias. Also, it looks very striking with purple foliage plants – for example, alternanthera.

Verbena
○ ❀ ❖ SUMMER to AUTUMN
H 45cm (18in)

Bedding verbenas are spreading plants with long, stiff stems carrying rounded heads of flowers in colours from white to dark purple and red, including bicolours and pastel shades. They are excellent for containers, particularly hanging baskets and window boxes, and combine well with most other container annuals, including sanvitalias, bidens, fuchsias and pelargoniums. Aztec series (shown above) is an early-flowering collection in many colours.

Viola 'Tiger Eyes'
○ ◐ ❖ SPRING to AUTUMN
H 15cm (6in)

There are many summer-flowering pansies in a wide range of colours, but this little plant is among the most attention-grabbing of the lot. It has old-gold petals, heavily marked with black veins that radiate from the dark centre. It looks good at the front of flower beds or in containers. Try combining it with dark colours to complement its markings, or with flowers in orange-yellow or gold shades.

Viola tricolor Heartsease

○ ◐ ❖ SPRING to AUTUMN

H 8–12cm (3–5in)

Often overlooked in the rush for large-flowered pansies, the little heartsease has many virtues: its small, delicate flowers with yellow 'faces' and violet 'wings' are produced for months on end on tiny plants that are content to grow nearly anywhere you put them. Plant them at the front of annual or perennial borders and around the edge of pots – they never look out of place.

Zinnia elegans 'Zahara'

○ ✿ ✕ ❖ SUMMER

H 30–50cm (12–20cm)

Zinnias are grown for their paintbox-bright flowers on slender stems. Despite their brightness, they are quite refined and blend well with other refined annuals, such as cosmos and cleome. You can also grow them with marigolds (*Tagetes*), dahlias and tithonias and get some astonishing results. 'Zahara' has single and double flowers in yellow, pink, white and red.

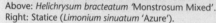
Everlasting flowers

Above: *Helichrysum bracteatum* 'Monstrosum Mixed'.
Right: Statice (*Limonium sinuatum* 'Azure').

Choosing everlasting flowers

Many annual flowers are perfect for drying for long-lasting floral displays; you can keep these indoors over winter to remind yourself of summer. Most also make very attractive garden plants and can be grown in flower beds among other annuals or used to fill gaps in perennial borders. Three of the most familiar are helichrysum, globe amaranth and statice, all of which you can grow easily from seed.

MORE ANNUALS SUITABLE FOR DRYING

Amaranthus caudatus (love-lies-bleeding)
Briza maxima (greater quaking grass)
Celosia Cockscomb varieties
Centaurea cyanus (cornflower)
Consolida ajacis (larkspur)
Lagurus ovatus (hare's tail grass)
Molucella laevis (bells of Ireland)
Nigella damascena seedheads (love-in-a-mist)
Papaver somniferum seedheads (opium poppy)
Pennisetum glaucum (ornamental millet)
Pennisetum setaceum (fountain grass)
Salvia viridis (clary)

Helichrysum or strawflower (sometimes known as *Bracteantha* or *Xerochrysum bracteatum, see* above) has flowers that are pretty much already dry: the petals feel crisp and smooth. The flowers are bright shades of pink, orange and yellow, often with a silvery overlay.

Globe amaranth (*Gomphrena globosa*) has magenta flowers that are rounded and from a distance look rather like clover.

Statice (*Limonium sinuatum, see* above) has quite small flowers at the top of 'winged' stems. Their colours include violets and blues as well as pink, yellow and white.

Harvesting everlasting flowers

Grow the plants in full sun and well-drained soil. Cut the flowers on a dry day. Pick those of statice when they are fully open and those of strawflower just before they open; globe amaranth stays as a cone shape, so pick it while it is still well coloured. Bring the flowers indoors to a cool, dark, dry place and hang them upside down in bunches to dry.

Summer foliage plants and grasses

Foliage plants and grasses are a great way to add an extra dimension to your borders and containers, and often last into autumn and beyond. Many foliage plants are perfect for creating a backdrop to highlight flower colours or to bring a soothing calm to very bright displays, but there are also those that are striking enough to be key players in a scheme. Grasses add structure, texture and a strong vertical element to displays.

Aeonium arboreum 'Atropurpureum'
◑ ✸ ❖ YEAR-ROUND
H 45–50cm (18–20in)

This striking, shrubby succulent is rather sculptural, with rosettes of bronze-purple, tongue-like leaves on thick stems. It should be planted where you can best appreciate its extraordinary appearance, such as in a pot or a raised bed. Create a contrast with orange or red flowers; a softer combination would be with silvery foliage. Bring it into a bright spot indoors from late autumn to spring. *Aeonium* 'Zwartkop' has nearly black leaves.

Alternanthera dentata 'Purple Knight' Joy weed
◯ ◑ ✸ ❖ SUMMER to MID-AUTUMN
H 50cm (20in)

The leaves of 'Purple Knight' are a glorious, deep burgundy colour, making this tender perennial a very striking, garden-worthy plant. It looks wonderful spilling over the edges of containers or planted in borders, and makes a good partner for hot-coloured flowers or for rich blues or pale pinks. The foliage colour looks best in full sun.

Artemisia 'Powis Castle'
◯ ❄ ❖ SUMMER to AUTUMN
H 60cm (24in)

This is a deservedly popular perennial with feathery, silver-grey foliage that adds sparkle to any planting. The leaves also give it a soft outline, making it perfect for combining with starchier plants, such as marigolds (*Tagetes*) and pelargoniums. Silver goes with most other colours, usually softening blues and purples and sharpening reds and oranges. *Artemisia ludoviciana* 'Silver Queen' has less deeply divided leaves.

Artemisia vulgaris 'Oriental Limelight'
◯ ◑ ❄ ❖ SUMMER to MID-AUTUMN
H 50cm (20in)

As well as being bright gold-and-green-variegated, the leaves of this perennial are deeply cut, making it useful for softening the edges of bedding plants that have stiff habits. It looks excellent with pink pelargoniums and plants with rich-violet or purple flowers or foliage. Try combining it with *Salvia guaranitica* 'Black and Blue' or *S. farinacea* 'Seascape', for example, or with the purple-leaved *Alternanthera dentata* 'Purple Knight'.

Briza maxima
Greater quaking grass
◯ ✗ ❖ SUMMER to AUTUMN
H 35–60cm (14–24in)

The pendent flowerheads of this slender grass appear in late spring and continue to ripen and grow well into autumn, by which time they are full of seeds and have faded to pale beige-brown, as has the whole plant. It looks good growing with wildflowers, such as cornflowers (*Centaurea*), poppies (*Papaver*) and love-in-a-mist (*Nigella*), in naturalistic drifts; alternatively, plant it among everlasting flowers. Grow from seed.

Canna 'Phasion'
○ ❁ ❖ SUMMER to LATE AUTUMN
H 1.2–2m (4–6ft)

If you like bright foliage on statuesque plants, you'll like this tender perennial (also known as 'Durban' or 'Tropicanna'). Its paddle-shaped leaves are dark green, striped with rich coppery orange and pink. The equally vivid autumn flowers are rich orange. If you have room, grow several, set off with other tall plants, like love-lies-bleeding (*Amaranthus caudatus*) or dahlias. Underplant with strongly shaped flowers such as osteospermums, marigolds (*Tagetes*) or salvias.

Canna 'Striata'
○ ❁ ❖ SUMMER to LATE AUTUMN
H 1.2–1.5m (4–5ft)

Bright green leaves with thin, yellow stripes and red stems characterize this tender perennial (also known as 'Pretoria'), making it an eye-catching focal point. It also has brilliant-orange autumn flowers. Dark bronze foliage or rich-red flowers contrast beautifully with the canna's strong lime colouring. It would look good with the castor oil plant *Ricinus communis* 'Carmencita' or dahlias such as 'Bishop of Llandaff'.

Dichondra argentea 'Silver Falls'
○ ◐ ◖ ❁ ❖ SUMMER to AUTUMN
H 90cm (3ft)

The long, trailing stems of this attractive little plant are thickly covered with small, silvery, heart-shaped leaves. If it is grown in open ground, the stems will take root and spread. It is ideal for hanging baskets and window boxes, quickly creating a dense screen, but can also be planted in any container or at the edge of a raised bed, beside steps and so on. It goes with almost any colour but looks particularly good with pink.

Ensete ventricosum 'Maurelii'
○ ◐ ❁ ❖ SUMMER to AUTUMN
H 2–2.2m (6–7ft)

This is a strongly architectural tender perennial that resembles a banana (*Musa*), with huge, paddle-shaped leaves of rich green heavily infused with red. The leaves look stunning with the evening sun shining through them; the plant is worth having just for this. Use it as a focal point in a large container – the rootball is relatively small – or in the ground. Protect it from winter cold if you want to keep it.

Euphorbia hypericifolia 'Diamond Frost'
○ ◐ ❁ ❖ SUMMER to AUTUMN
H 30–60cm (12–24in)

With its spindly stems carrying narrow, rich-green leaves, this plant is intriguing enough, but add the cloud of tiny, white 'flowers' (actually bracts) above them and it is irresistible. It is lovely on its own in a container or as a foil to bigger flowers, such as petunias. In borders, combine it with upright plants such as salvias or grasses. The variety 'Breathless Blush' has leaves with bronze markings.

Glechoma hederacea 'Variegata'
○ ◐ ❖ SUMMER to AUTUMN
H 1–1.2m (40–48in)

This perennial trailer has long stems of rounded leaves with scalloped edges highlighted in white. In summer it produces pale mauve flowers, but these are not its main attraction. Instead, it is the pretty foliage that is in demand for decorating the edges of containers, especially hanging baskets and window boxes. It is rather a coarse plant, but the variegation gives it some sophistication and it goes well with pale busy lizzies (*Impatiens*) or petunias.

Helichrysum petiolare 'Limelight'

○ ⬡ pH↓ ❖ SUMMER to AUTUMN
H 60–90cm (2–3ft)

The softly hairy, yellow-green leaves of this trailing shrub make a valuable contribution to many summer pots and hanging baskets. The stems arch outwards and upwards, giving it a more lively appearance than some trailers. Use it with soft pinks or blues as well as with hotter shades like orange-red and rich yellow. The species, *Helichrysum petiolare,* has silver-grey leaves.

Lagurus ovatus Hare's tail grass

○ ✂ ❖ SUMMER to EARLY AUTUMN
H 40–50cm (16–20in)

A delightful little grass, hare's tail has unremarkable grassy leaves but its fluffy, oval flowerheads are attractive and very touchable, too. They start green and gradually turn cream to buff-brown as the seeds ripen. Plant it among low-growing informal annuals, such as California poppy (*Eschscholzia californica*) and love-in-a-mist (*Nigella*), or use it to fill gaps in perennial borders. Raise from seed.

Ophiopogon planiscapus 'Nigrescens' Lilyturf

○ ◑ pH↓ ❖ YEAR ROUND
H 10cm (4in)

The nearly black leaves of this grassy perennial have led to it becoming a bit of a designer speciality. However, its very dark foliage can make it disappear, much like a black hole in space, so it needs paler surroundings – even just a gravel mulch or light container – to be seen at its best. Plant it with white or pale pink flowers: cyclamen in winter and busy lizzies (*Impatiens*) in summer.

Ipomoea 'Black Tone'
Sweet potato

○ ◑ ⬡ ❖ SUMMER to AUTUMN
H 10–25cm (4–10in)

A relative of the edible sweet potato, this elegant little vine has heart-shaped, nearly black leaves. It is perfect for adding an air of sophistication to hanging baskets and around the edges of other containers. Plant it with white-flowered busy lizzies (*Impatiens*) or pelargoniums to create something classy, or use it with pink nemesia or diascia for a softer effect. 'Blackie' is similar but with more divided leaves.

Lotus berthelotii Parrot's beak

○ ⬡ ❖ SUMMER to AUTUMN
H 30–45cm (12–18in)

This tender perennial, mainly valued for its trailing foliage, has long, thin leaves in whorls on pendent stems. Ranging from silver- to blue-green, they create a wonderful foil for the red flowers, which may appear in summer, given steadily hot, dry weather and a sheltered spot. Use it in hanging baskets and around the rims of containers. It looks good with red or orange-red flowers.

Oxalis triangularis Wood sorrel

○ ◑ ❖ SUMMER to MID-AUTUMN
H 18cm (7in)

Although grown primarily for its sumptuously rich, two-toned purple leaves, this wood sorrel also has pretty, pale pink flowers above the foliage in summer. For a brilliant contrast, grow it with a silver-foliage plant, such as *Senecio cineraria*, or use it as a foil to orange-flowered busy lizzies (*Impatiens*) or calibrachoas. It also looks good with bluish-pink flowers, which complement its flowers and foliage.

Pelargonium 'Lady Plymouth'

○ ◐ ❋ pH↑ ❖ SUMMER to AUTUMN

H 30–40cm (12–16in)

Some pelargoniums, known as scented-leaved, are grown for the extraordinary fragrance of their foliage. They usually have small flowers in shades of white, pink or mauve. 'Lady Plymouth' (above) has deeply divided, white-edged leaves and a strong eau-de-cologne scent. 'Graveolens' is lemony; 'Attar of Roses' is rose-scented. Crush a leaf each time you pass by. (*See also* page 73.)

Pennisetum glaucum 'Purple Majesty' Ornamental millet

○ ❋ ❖ LATE SPRING to AUTUMN

H 90cm (3ft)

The leaves of this architectural perennial grass are dark purple-black, as are the stiff, rather fat spikes of flowers. It has an upright habit, giving it a regal air in flower beds or containers. Try it with yellow or red rudbeckias, gaillardias, shortish sunflowers (*Helianthus*) and other daisy-like flowers for a prairie effect, or combine it with pale pinks and blues for something more refined.

Perilla frutescens

○ ◐ ❋ ❖ SUMMER to AUTUMN

H 60–90cm (2–3ft)

Tall and with leaves not unlike a stinging nettle's in shape but bronze-purple in colour, perilla is a traditional 'dot' plant. It is also a good foliage plant for borders or containers. Grow it with bright orange flowers, such as pot marigolds (*Calendula*), for an eye-catching display; alternatively, if you would prefer a cooler look, try combining it with soft magenta and pale pink ones, such as spider flower (*Cleome spinosa*) or phlox.

Pelargonium 'Vancouver Centennial'

○ ◐ ❋ pH↑ ❖ SUMMER to AUTUMN

H 25–30cm (10–12in)

The leaves of this zonal pelargonium are extremely eye-catching. Fresh green with heavy, dark red-brown flushing, they are also deeply cut, giving them a sculptural quality. The flat, single flowers are red-orange, and the petals have a matching jagged edge. Grow it on its own in a pot in a prime position or try it with soft-leaved plants, such as the grass *Stipa tenuissima*. (*See also* page 73.)

Pennisetum setaceum 'Rubrum' Fountain grass

○ ❄ ❖ LATE SPRING to AUTUMN

H 90cm (3ft)

Everyone covets this perennial grass for its lovely mound of burgundy-red foliage and, in late summer, its similarly coloured, fluffy flowerheads that fade to beige. Grow it in a pot on its own, or in borders with red dahlias, ricinus and cannas. For more contrast, place it among yellow flowers, like rudbeckias, and lime-green foliage. 'Fireworks' has red-and-white-variegated leaves.

Plectranthus madagascariensis 'Variegated Mintleaf' Mintleaf

○ ◐ ❋ ❖ SUMMER to AUTUMN

H 30–50cm (12–20in)

This trailing perennial is grown for its toothed, variegated leaves, which smell of mint when bruised. The leaves are carried on stiff, sturdy, square stems that will creep and root if the plant is grown in the open ground. It is useful for providing a good foliage backdrop for flowering trailers in containers, and combines particularly well with verbenas in soft blues and dusky reds.

Ricinus communis 'Carmencita'
Castor oil plant

◯ ❋ ❖ SUMMER to MID-AUTUMN

H 2–2.5m (6–8ft) or more

The huge, dark red leaves of this striking tender shrub are primarily what it's grown for, although it does also have attractive red, fluffy-looking flowers. It looks tropical and is stunning with other large foliage plants, such as cannas and grasses. Combine it with orange or red dahlias too, as well as taller red salvias and tithonias.

Senecio cineraria 'Silver Dust'

◯ ❋ ❖ SUMMER to AUTUMN

H 30cm (12in)

Very divided leaves make this shrubby annual (also called *Cineraria maritima*) look almost coral-like, and their silver to near-white colour ensures it is eye-catching. It is suitable for containers and the front of borders and combines well with pinks, purples and blues; use it with reds and oranges if you want something with more zing. Its yellow flowers are often removed. 'Cirrus' is similar, but the leaves are much less divided.

Solenostemon
Coleus, Painted nettle

◯ ◐ ❋ ❖ SUMMER to MID-AUTUMN

H 50–60cm (20–24in)

Coleus is a tender perennial with leaves ranging from lime green to deep dark brown-red with mottles, flares, edges and stripes in complementary or contrasting colours, including red, pink and white. It is effective *en masse* in a hot border and is a good companion for a range of plants in containers. Good varieties include 'Dark Chocolate' (shown above) and 'Kong Rose' (green leaves with bleeding, dark red centres).

Stipa tenuissima

◯ ❖ SUMMER to WINTER

H 60cm (24in)

One of the loveliest of all small foliage plants, this perennial grass (also known as *Nassella*) forms a neat, dense tuft of narrow leaves that stir in the breeze and just ask to be stroked. It is ideal for adding soft texture in borders and looks particularly good with daisy-like flowers, such as rudbeckias or osteospermums, or with wildflowers: for instance, poppies (*Papaver*) and cornflowers (*Centaurea*).

Strobilanthes dyeriana
Persian shield

◯ ◐ ❋ ❖ SUMMER to AUTUMN

H 80–90cm (32–36in)

This lovely tender shrub has long, pointed, narrow leaves that are a rich purple colour, darker underneath, with a silver shimmer, making them look almost metallic. It is wonderful as a feature plant in a pot and also for growing with soft-pink flowers, such as cosmos and clarkias. Try it with red too, perhaps rich-red opium poppies (*Papaver somniferum*) or dahlias.

Tanacetum ptarmiciflorum
Pyrethrum

◯ ❋ ❖ SUMMER to AUTUMN

H 60–90cm (24–36in)

Not unlike *Senecio cineraria* 'Silver Dust' in appearance, this is a softly felted, spreading perennial with finely cut, filigree leaves. It is suitable for the edges of flower beds and containers. Use it in combination with pastel diascias and argyranthemums for a cool display, or add heat with the orange, rust and red end of the spectrum.

Summer-flowering climbers

Annual climbers are among the most useful plants in a garden for filling gaps and for providing height and colour. If you don't want them to climb up, most are happy to cascade down and a few will also scramble along and over, either the ground or other plants. There are vividly coloured varieties and more stylish ones – something for all tastes. Always try to include one or two in your summer garden.

Cobaea scandens
Cup and saucer vine
○ ◑ ❀ ❖ SUMMER to AUTUMN
H 4–6m (13–20ft) or more

This is a vigorous tender perennial vine with dark green leaves made of oval leaflets and with a tendril at the end for clinging. The large, thick-textured, scented flowers are creamy when they open, darkening to purple. Grow this substantial vine where it can scramble as far as it wants and where you can appreciate the flowers: you don't always get all that many, but they are gorgeous. Grow from seed.

Eccremocarpus scaber
Chilean glory flower
○ ❈ ❖ SUMMER to AUTUMN
H 3m (10ft) or more

Ideal for growing through another climber, such as black-eyed susan (*Thunbergia alata*) or over a shrub or small tree, this spindly vine has square stems and dark green leaves divided into small leaflets. The tubular flowers are produced in slender groups at the end of the stems. The blooms are quite small but their orange-red colour makes them very eye-catching. Grow from seed.

Ipomoea lobata Spanish flag
○ ❈ ❖ SUMMER to AUTUMN
H 2–3m (6–10ft) or more

Spanish flag is a fast-growing tender perennial climber with three-lobed leaves and purple-flushed stems. Its flowers open dark red and fade to yellow then cream. They face one way on the stems, creating a 'flag' effect. This is quite a substantial plant and looks good on its own, scrambling over trellis or a wall; it also goes well with black-eyed susan (*Thunbergia alata*) and morning glory (*Ipomoea tricolor*). Grow from seed.

Ipomoea tricolor
'Heavenly Blue' Morning glory
○ ❈ ❖ SUMMER
H 3–4m (10–12ft)

The beautiful large trumpet flowers of morning glory welcome every morning in tropical climes, but we must content ourselves with enjoying them only in the summer. Plant this vine where it can scramble uninhibited – sheltered from strong winds – and where you can appreciate the rich-green, heart-shaped leaves as well as the flowers. Each flower lasts only a day, but there are always more to come. Grow from seed.

Lathyrus Incense Mix
Sweet pea
○ ◑ ✕ ❖ SUMMER to EARLY AUTUMN
H 2m (6ft) or more

There are many sweet pea varieties in all sorts of colours and often scented, but this selection has been made specifically for the perfume. The flowers are soft pastel shades of lilac, pink and peach and, as with all sweet peas, the more you pick, the more you get. Grow them over a wigwam of bamboo canes or a hazel obelisk and tie them in. Grow from seed.

Lathyrus 'Painted Lady'
Sweet pea
○ ◑ ⋏ ❖ EARLY SUMMER to EARLY AUTUMN
H 2m (6ft) or more

This sweet pea has been around for 200 years – a good recommendation. It starts to produce its heavily scented, bicoloured pink-and-white flowers in early summer. For the earliest flowers on strong plants, sow them in autumn and keep in a sheltered place in winter. They look superb with cottage-garden annuals such as clary (*Salvia viridis*), love-in-a-mist (*Nigella*), pot marigolds (*Calendula*) and poppies (*Papaver*).

Lophospermum erubescens
Creeping gloxinia, Lofos
○ ❖ SUMMER to AUTUMN
H 0.6–2m (2–6ft)

Although often grown in hanging baskets, this tender perennial climber can go upwards if desired. It has pale green, three-lobed leaves with heavily serrated edges and tubular flowers, rich purple-red in 'Burgundy Falls' (shown above) and creamy white in 'Summer Cream'. It looks lovely on its own in a hanging basket, but could be joined by busy lizzies (*Impatiens*) or pelargoniums.

Rhodochiton atrosanguineus
Purple bell vine
○ ❖ SUMMER to AUTUMN
H 2–3m (6–10ft)

This fragile-looking tender perennial has pendent, maroon-purple flowers opening from pink buds that remain cap-like over the flower. The leaves are heart-shaped, sometimes with purple tints. It's a stunner when draped over a slender support, underplanted with pink or purple busy lizzies (*Impatiens*) or a silver-foliage plant like *Dichondra* 'Silver Falls'. It is also striking with a contrasting foliage plant (here, *Canna* 'Striata').

Thunbergia alata
Black-eyed susan
○ ❖ SUMMER to AUTUMN
H 1.2–2m (4–6ft)

With vigorous, twining stems swathed in long, triangular leaves, this tender perennial vine soon covers an obelisk or a wigwam. Its round-faced flowers are orange or yellow with a dark centre. 'African Sunset' (shown above) is soft-coloured, with flowers ranging from rich brick-red to apricot-orange, colours that would combine well with blues and purples like those found in verbenas and petunias. Give it a sheltered site.

Tropaeolum majus
Tip Top series Nasturtium
○ ❖ SUMMER to AUTUMN
H to 1.5m (5ft)

Nasturtiums are among those plants children are encouraged to grow, since they are so easy and have such bright colours. Tip Top series is a good example of a wide colour selection, with shades that appeal to both children and adults, including 'Mahogany' (shown above), 'Apricot' and 'Scarlet'. Grow them all in poor soil for more flowers and fewer leaves. Easy to grow from seed.

Tropaeolum peregrinum
Canary creeper
○ ❖ SUMMER to AUTUMN
H 2.5–3m (8–10ft) or more

This is a vigorous climber with five-lobed, grey-green leaves and clear yellow flowers that look rather like tiny birds. It is a lovely plant and slightly more elegant than its relative *Tropaeolum majus* (nasturtium). Plant it against a fence or wall and underplant with lupins, blue salvias and opium poppies (*Papaver somniferum*). Grow from seed.

Autumn and winter

Autumn is a wonderful time in the garden, frequently with unexpected weeks of warmth, allowing summer plants to keep on going. In winter, the bright foliage of evergreens comes to the fore, and a few brave flowers provide spots of colour, too. There are several shrubs and miniature trees that, while they are young, can be used in containers or to add structure in the instant-colour garden. Many are sold in tiny sizes. Some can be used year after year in pots; others will get too large eventually, so you'll need to transfer them to the garden or the compost heap.

Brassica oleracea
Ornamental cabbage
○ pH ↑ ❖ AUTUMN AND WINTER
H 30–45cm (12–18in)

Although rather strange-looking, ornamental cabbages have proved popular for containers and formal bedding and are valuable for providing long-lasting colour through the darkest months. For something eye-catching, plant them with yellow or blue grasses, such as *Carex* and *Festuca glauca*. They also combine well with cyclamen.

Carex oshimensis 'Evergold'
○ ◑ ❖ YEAR-ROUND
H 25–30cm (10–12in)

The bright yellow leaves of this striking evergreen sedge are clearly defined by their narrow, dark green margins, giving the plant an almost sculptural look, which is even more marked if it has a dark companion such as coprosma. It can be grown in a dampish border or in a container and provides a bright foil for magenta flowers, such as cyclamen, or the soft-red berries of gaultheria.

Ajuga reptans Bugle
○ ◑ ❖ YEAR-ROUND
H 15–30cm (6–12in)

There are several perennial bugles that are grown mainly for their evergreen foliage; an added bonus is that they produce short spikes of blue flowers in late spring and early summer. Good varieties include 'Black Scallop' (shown above, very dark leaves) and 'Burgundy Glow' (silver-green leaves with reddish tints). Grow them in containers or at the front of borders, using paler foliage plants to highlight their colours.

Calluna vulgaris Garden Girls series Ling, Scots heather
○ pH ↓ ❖ MIDSUMMER to LATE AUTUMN
H 30–45cm (12–18in)

This is a specially selected collection of 'bud-blooming' heathers. This means the flowers never open fully and are, therefore, not pollinated, so they last for ages without fading. They are ideal for pots (use ericaceous compost) combined with foliage plants, such as euonymus and *Cupressus macrocarpa* 'Goldcrest'. Good varieties include: 'Alexandra' (rich red-pink), 'Alicia' (white), 'Amethyst' (above, crimson-purple) and 'Larissa' (pale pink). (*See also* page 88.)

Chamaecyparis lawsoniana 'Ellwoodii'
○ pH ↓ ❖ YEAR-ROUND
H 20–90cm (8–36in), eventually more

This slow-growing conifer is small and slender when young, with upward-pointing, blue-grey branches. A shapely focal point in a large container, it is a foil for red berries, flowers and foliage – for example, those of gaultheria, skimmia or heuchera. It also looks good with daffodils and crocuses in spring. It can be used for many years in a pot; trim lightly if necessary to keep it compact. 'Ellwood's Gold' is a similar shape but greener with a warm gold flush.

Chrysanthemum 'Lynn'

○ ❄ ❖ SUMMER to AUTUMN
H to 50cm (20in)

Bedding chrysanthemums appear in garden centres just when you don't expect to see any more showy flowers until spring. They are usually smothered in blooms in a wide variety of colours, including white, yellow, bronze-orange and cerise. 'Lynn' is a particularly attractive, dark-centred pink variety and can be grown with red fruit or foliage, such as gaultherias or coprosmas, or something more silvery, like festucas.

Coprosma repens 'Pacific Night'

○ ◐ ❀ ❖ YEAR-ROUND
H 1m (40in)

This somewhat tender, bushy shrub is grown for its smallish, glossy, deep purple-brown leaves, which make it an excellent backdrop for an autumn and winter container in a sheltered spot. Don't crush the leaves, since they smell rather unpleasant. The foliage looks best with a paler or brighter partner, so choose pink, red or yellow flowers, such as chrysanthemums, cyclamen or even winter-flowering primroses (Primula).

Cupressus macrocarpa 'Goldcrest'

○ ◐ ❖ YEAR-ROUND
H 15–90cm (6–36in), eventually more

This slender, pale yellow-green conifer makes a lovely container plant for a year or two (until it grows very tall) and is often seen in winter pots with heathers and heaths, ivy (Hedera), skimmia and cyclamen. Also, try it with heucheras and Carex oshimensis 'Evergold', and irises and daffodils in spring. Shelter the conifer from cold winds.

Cyclamen persicum
Florist's cyclamen

○ ◐ ❀ ❖ AUTUMN to MIDWINTER
H 20cm (8in)

This cyclamen, which flowers in the depth of winter, is often sold as an indoor plant. However, it is also suitable outdoors in mild sites – for instance, in a window box in a city centre. It comes in rich cerise, red, pale pink and white; some also have a sweet scent. Large-flowered types include Halios and Sierra series; the Onduel and Miracle series ('Flame Mixed' is shown above) are much smaller. Both look good with evergreens, such as euonymus and ivy.

Erica × darleyensis 'Kramer's Rote'

○ ◐ pH↓ ❖ LATE WINTER to EARLY SPRING
H 30cm (12in)

Erica × darleyensis varieties are all worth having through the winter for their flowers and their evergreen foliage (*see* page 88). 'Kramer's Rote' is particularly attractive because of its bronze-green foliage – a dark backdrop for its urn-shaped, purple-pink flowers. Plant it at the edge of containers with coprosma, ivies (Hedera) and other evergreens. In spring, add anemones and irises.

Euonymus fortunei 'Emerald 'n' Gold'

○ ◐ ❖ YEAR-ROUND
H 60–120cm (2–4ft), eventually more

This evergreen shrub with oval, slightly leathery leaves will trail or, given encouragement, climb. It is an ideal permanent feature for a winter container, when its yellow-margined leaves may tinge pink. It looks good with other evergreens and is effective for adding texture to displays of spring bulbs and other bedding. 'Emerald Gaiety' has bright green leaves with white margins, pink-tinged in winter.

Above left: *Erica carnea* 'Myretoun Ruby'. Top right: *Erica carnea* f. *albiflora* 'Springwood White'. Bottom right: *Calluna vulgaris* 'Crimson Glory'.

Choosing heathers and heaths

Heathers (*Calluna*) and heaths (*Erica*) make good temporary container plants and are often used as ground cover. They are small evergreen shrubs, 15–30cm (6–12in) tall, with slender, upright branches covered in tiny leaves and little bell- or urn-shaped flowers. The foliage varies from very dark green to bright lime-gold; the brighter colours often change with the time of year. The flowers, which are fairly long-lasting, are in shades of pink, purple, lilac and cerise or white, sometimes darker around their mouths.

Heathers and heaths are very similar in appearance. Heathers have scale-like, overlapping leaves and flower from late summer to mid-autumn; heaths have needle-like foliage and bloom between late winter and early spring, making them extremely valuable for colour late in the year, when little else is around.

Growing heathers and heaths

Heathers need acid soil, and while most heaths also prefer acid soil, some (*Erica carnea, E. × darleyensis*) tolerate slightly alkaline conditions. If you're growing them in a pot, choose ericaceous compost for the best results. Most need a sunny position, but *E. carnea* will grow and flower in shade, too. Trim them with shears after flowering. They can remain in a pot for a year or two; after this, plant them in the ground.

GOOD HEATHERS AND HEATHS

Calluna vulgaris 'Crimson Glory' (*see* above) – pale purple flowers; foliage golden becoming orange then red.

C. vulgaris Garden Girls series (*see* page 86) – pink, purple or white flowers.

C. vulgaris 'Peter Sparks' – double, rose-pink flowers.

Erica carnea f. *albiflora* 'Springwood White' (*see* above) – trailing habit; white flowers; bright green foliage.

E. carnea 'King George' – flowers very early in winter; deep-pink flowers.

E. carnea 'Myretoun Ruby' (*see* above) – flowers pink becoming crimson.

E. × darleyensis 'Silberschmelze' – white flowers; deep green foliage tipped red in winter, cream in spring.

E. × darleyensis 'Kramer's Rote' (*see* page 87) – purple-pink flowers; bronze-green foliage.

Euonymus japonicus 'Pierrolino'

○ ◐ ❖ YEAR-ROUND

H 75cm (30in)

With an upright habit and very heavily white-mottled young leaves, this lovely compact shrub is ideal for adding a little light to an autumn and winter container and makes a good feature plant in winter bedding schemes. The leaves become darker and are eventually deep green when mature. This plant looks particularly good with warmer colours, such as skimmias, gaultherias, heathers, heaths or heucheras. It will survive happily in a container for many years.

Festuca glauca 'Elijah Blue'

○ ❖ YEAR-ROUND

H 30cm (12in)

One of those designer plants often used to create tasteful monochrome displays, 'Elijah Blue' is a tufty perennial grass with narrow, blue-grey foliage that has a silvery tint. It also produces tall, grassy flower spikes in summer and these fade to an attractive beige-brown. Combine it with warm pinks and purples, such as gaultherias or heucheras. 'Blaufuchs' ('Blue Fox') is similar but a little bluer.

Gaultheria Pernettya
○ ◐ pH ↓ ❖ YEAR-ROUND
H 15–90cm (6–36in), eventually more

With their cheery berries set against dark green leaves, these evergreen shrubs are excellent for winter containers; the pink or white, late-spring and early-summer flowers are an added bonus. Try them with golden sedge (*Carex oshimensis* 'Evergold') and ornamental cabbages (*Brassica*). Good varieties (all H 15–25cm/ 6–10in) include: *G. mucronata* 'Mulberry Wine' (magenta, shown above) and 'Wintertime' (white); *G. procumbens* has aromatic leaves and scarlet fruit.

Helichrysum italicum 'Korma' Curry plant
○ pH ↑ ❖ YEAR-ROUND
H 15–40cm (6–16in)

Even if you're not familiar with this shrub, you'll recognize its strong, curry-spice aroma that will carry quite a way. It has upright branches clad in long, silvery leaves, a bit like those of lavender. In a pot, combine it with winter pansies and primulas, in bright reds and oranges; alternatively, plant it with the black-leaved, grass-like *Ophiopogon planiscapus* 'Nigrescens' for something more refined.

Heuchera 'Plum Pudding'
○ ◐ ❖ YEAR-ROUND
H 25cm (10in)

One of many purple-leaved heucheras (*see also* page 90), 'Plum Pudding' is valuable for its evergreen leaves, which are dark burgundy with a strong metallic sheen. A resilient plant, withstanding most winter weather, it produces slender spikes of white flowers on purple stems in spring. Use it in elegant winter containers with silver leaves, such as those of the curry plant (*Helichrysum italicum* 'Korma'), or the pale-flowered Christmas rose (*Helleborus niger*).

Hedera helix Common ivy
○ ◐ ● ❖ YEAR-ROUND
H 50cm–1.2m (20in–4ft)

Ivies can spread afar, but most make good container plants for a year or so. Smaller versions of perennial common ivy, such as 'Glacier' (shown above) and 'Eva' (similar, with a longer central leaf lobe), seldom get too rampant. Their trailing habit and soft-grey colouring with splashes of cream and white make them perfect with almost any other plant in an autumn and winter display.

Helleborus niger Christmas rose
○ ◐ ❖ EARLY WINTER to EARLY SPRING
H 30cm (12in)

This lovely perennial has long-lasting, large, bowl-shaped flowers, usually white but sometimes with a pink tint. Its attractive leaves are divided into up to nine leaflets; they are often removed as the blooms develop to allow the flowers to show themselves off. In pots it looks good with skimmias, gaultherias and grasses such as festuca, and, later, with early-flowering *Cyclamen coum*.

Juniperus communis 'Compressa'
○ ◐ ❖ YEAR-ROUND
H 15–90cm (6–36in)

This neat, tiny conifer has a narrow, upright habit (it's about 20cm/8in wide), and as a slow grower is happy in a container for several years. The prickly, blue-green to blue-grey foliage looks good with purple-red or pink flowers or foliage. Grow it as a permanent plant in a pot, adding heucheras, heaths (*Erica*) and ivies (*Hedera*) in winter, bulbs in spring, and low-growing bedding in summer.

Heuchera

Left: *Heuchera* 'Mint Frost'.
Right: *Heuchera* 'Licorice'.

Choosing heucheras

Mainly valued as foliage plants, heucheras are low-growing evergreen perennials – around 20–25cm (8–10in) high when not in flower – and form mounds of rounded, lobed leaves in shades ranging from pale yellow-greens, though custard and caramel to rich deep purple and nearly black, with or without silver overlays and darker veins. Some varieties also have ruffling on the leaf edges or the foliage is wavy rather than relatively flat. Heucheras produce pretty but tiny flowers on tall, slender stems, 40–45cm (16–18in) or more high, in late spring and early summer. Sometimes fairly inconspicuous, they are often white or pink but may be brightly coloured.

The number of varieties available to gardeners has increased enormously in recent years and there is now a heuchera for every situation.

Growing heucheras

Heucheras prefer moist, well-drained soil that is reasonably fertile. They grow in sun or partial shade and will even put up with deep shade provided they get enough water. Although they are more or less evergreen, those that are in the garden usually have a dormant period in winter, so if you want winter colour, you'll need to buy plants in leaf at the time. In the garden they make good ground cover and look particularly spectacular *en masse*, but in a mixed container just one will be sufficient to make its mark.

GOOD HEUCHERA VARIETIES

Heuchera 'Caramel' – rich pink-yellow leaves; creamy flowers.

H. 'Crème Brûlée' – copper, amber and pink leaves; soft-pink flowers.

H. 'Ebony and Ivory' – dark near-black leaves; white flowers.

H. 'Georgia Peach' – salmon-pink, silvery leaves; white flowers.

H. 'Key Lime Pie' – lime-green leaves, which are yellower in summer; rose-pink flowers.

H. 'Licorice' (*see above*) – near-black leaves with a hint of purple-red; white flowers.

H. 'Lipstick' – rich-green leaves with silver overlay; bright red flowers.

H. 'Mint Frost' (*see above*) – mint-green leaves with a silver sheen and red-brown veins; cream flowers.

H. 'Peach Flambé' – peachy-pink leaves, darker in winter; white flowers.

H. 'Plum Pudding' (*see* page 89) – burgundy leaves; white flowers.

Leucothoe 'Scarletta'

◑ ● pH ↓ ❖ YEAR-ROUND

H 30–60cm (12–24in), eventually more

For a bit of winter colour, there is little to beat this small evergreen shrub. Its branches arch slightly outwards, giving it a soft outline, and they are covered with long, oval leaves, warm bronze in winter. The young leaves are darker and in summer they are rich green. It makes a lovely specimen in a container, but is equally good combined with other plants, particularly heathers or heaths.

Picea glauca var. albertiana 'Conica'

○ pH ↓ ❖ YEAR-ROUND

H 1m (40in), eventually more

With its distinctive cone-shape, this chubby, soft-green conifer has spirals of needle-like leaves. It makes a lovely specimen in a big container, attractive on its own but also looking good with other plants around its base. In winter, select warm red tints, such as heucheras, heathers and heaths or cyclamen, and in spring and summer add bright flowering plants, including pansies and petunias.

Primula Bonneli series
○ ◑ ❖ EARLY to MIDWINTER
H 10–15cm (4–6in)

This is one of a number of collections of hybrid primulas that have been developed for flowering from early winter onwards. They are available in a range of fresh, bright colours including cream, yellow, red, violet, orange and bicoloured. All are reliable performers that flower for a long period and are perfect for slipping into pots among more permanent foliage plants.

Skimmia japonica
◑ ● ❖ WINTER to SPRING
H 15–100cm (6–40in), eventually more

Skimmias are versatile shrubs, and there are several different varieties that are worth growing for their winter buds and berries as well as their foliage and white spring flowers. Those mentioned are fine in a container for at least one winter. 'Fructo Albo' has green buds and white berries. 'Magic Marlot' has variegated foliage and white then red buds. 'Rubella' (shown above) has red-edged leaves and dark red buds.

Viola Rocky series
○ ◑ ❖ SPRING, AUTUMN, WINTER
H 8–10cm (3–4in)

If you want enormous amounts of colour over many months from low-maintenance plants, these violas are to be recommended. They are smothered in small, violet-like flowers in a choice of 36 colours. Pure shades include yellow, white and lilac, while bicolours include yellow with purple 'wings' (top petals) and red with a yellow face; some have imaginative names, such as 'Sunny Side Up' (shown above).

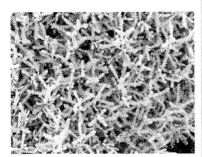

Santolina chamaecyparissus
Cotton lavender
○ ❖ YEAR-ROUND
H 15–50cm (6–20in)

Although it prefers the warm, dry climate of the Mediterranean, this little evergreen shrub performs well in Britain, too. It is grown for its aromatic, silver foliage, which looks good for most of the year and provides a bright reminder of summer in the depths of winter. Grow it as a foliage backdrop plant in a pot or use it – neatly clipped – for a formal winter bedding scheme.

Viola Endurio series
○ ◑ ❖ SPRING, SUMMER, WINTER
H 30–35cm (12–14in)

This semi-trailing plant has masses of pretty, violet-like flowers almost all year, depending on when you buy the plants: those on sale in autumn bloom in winter and spring, while those on sale in spring flower through summer. The varieties are named after their colours, which include pure yellow, yellow with violet 'wings' (top petals), yellow with red 'wings', lavender and sky blue. 'Tricolor' (shown above) is a colour mixture.

Thuja occidentalis 'Rheingold'
○ ❖ YEAR-ROUND
H 20–90cm (8–36in)

A cone-shaped conifer with golden-yellow leaves that are warmly pink-tinted when young, 'Rheingold' makes a handsome, permanent specimen in a large container. It is also suitable as a foil for many other foliage plants, including ivies (*Hedera*), leucothoes, heucheras and heathers and heaths. Brighten its lower regions with primulas, irises and other bulbs in spring and drape the delicate climber *Rhodochiton atrosanguineus* around it in summer.

Index

Page numbers in *italics* refer to plants in the Recommended bedding plants directory.

Acknowledgements

BBC Books and OutHouse would like to thank the following for
their assistance in preparing this book: Andy McIndoe for advice and
guidance; Robin Whitecross for picture research; Ruth Baldwin for
proofreading; Marie Lorimer for the index.

Picture credits

Key t = top, b = bottom, l = left, r = right, c = centre

PHOTOGRAPHS

All photographs by Jonathan Buckley (including 27 in conjunction
with the National Trust) unless listed below.

Ball Horticultural 21a, 21c, 21h, 22, 41br(1) & (5), 41cl(1) & (3),
41tl(3), (4) & (5), 41tr(5), bl(5) & cr(4), 57tr, 59tc, 60tr, 61bc & 61tr,
62bl & br, 63tl, tc, bc & tr, 64tc, 65tc, 68tc, 69tc & br, 71bl, 72tl &
br, 74tc & bc, 76tc, 77tc & bc, 78bl, 79tc, 80tc, 82tc, 83tc, 91tl

GAP Photos Lee Avison 76tr; BBC Magazines Ltd 74tl; Pernilla
Bergdahl 41br(2), 68bl, 72tc, 75tl, 86tc; BIOS 79l; Richard Bloom
41bl(2), 58tl, 81br, 90tr; Christina Bollen 35r, 72bl; Mark Bolton 73tc;
Elke Borkowski 29r, 42bl, 43, 62bc, 69tl; Leigh Clapp 61tl; Simon
Colmer 64br; Marg Cousens 59bl; Sarah Cuttle 70bl; Paul Debois
70tr; Carole Drake 41cl(4) & tr(1), 62tc, 67bc & tr, 88bc, 90br;
Heather Edwards 78tc; Ron Evans 58bl; FhF Greenmedia 17(3), 32b,
61br, 71bc, 91tr; Geoff du Feu 60bl; GAP Photos 39b; Susie Gibbons
11, 33; John Glover 4, 58br, 60tl, 70tl, 74br, 82tl; Anne Green-
Armytage 41cr(1), 63bl; Charles Hawes 39tr, 71tc; Marcus Harpur
80bl; Neil Holmes 26(2), 41tl(1); Martin Hughes-Jones 31(4), 60bc,
61bl, 66tr, 67br, 74bl; Dianna Jazwinski 81tc; Lynn Keddie 69bl, 87tc;
Geoff Kidd 41cr(5), 65tr, 79tr, 91br; Fiona Lea 30t, 70tc, 77tr; Gerald
Majumdar 70bc; Clive Nichols 9b, 20c, 39tl, 73tl & br; Howard Rice
39tc; JS Sira 41br(3), 64tl, 75bc, 77tl, 79bc, 82br, 83bl, 85br, 87tl;
Martin Staffler 15; S & O 26(1), 65bc, 75tc, 76bl; Friedrich Strauss
2/3, 19t, 34t, 38b, 41tr(4), 70br, 80br; Graham Strong 42t, 80bc,
86bc; Maddie Thornhill 62tr; Visions 41bl(4), 71tl & tr, 76tl, 91bc;
Juliette Wade 26(3), 66tl; Dave Zubraski 78tr

Garden Collection Derek Harris 13, Nicola Stocken Tomkins 38t, 75tr

GardenPhotos.com Judy White 84br

Garden Picture Library/Getty Images Andrea Jones 71br

Garden World Images Isabelle Anderson 41bl(1); Nicholas Appleby
41bl(3); Dr Alan Beaumont 67bl; Rita Coates 20h, 65tl, 66tc, 85tl,
89tr; Oscar D'arcy 68bc; Gilles Delacroix 41tr(2) & cr(3), 73tr, 80tr,
81bl, 83br, 85bl; Martin Hughes-Jones 19b, 20b, 56, 91tc; Andrea
Jones 42bc; Nicole et Patrick Mioulane 29l, 66br; MAP/Nathalie
Pasquel 41tr(3), 86br, 87bl; MAP/Nicole et Patrick Mioulane 88tr;
Jonathan Need 89br; Richard Shiell 41tl(2), 63br, 77br; Trevor Sims
60br, 68tr, 72bc, 87tr; Lee Thomas 16l, 83tr, 87bc; Don Wildridge
41cl(5), 81tl

Andrew McIndoe 17(2), 20d & g, 21f, & g, 41cl(2), 58tc, 59bc & tr,
61tc, 67tl, 82bl, 86l, 89bl, 90tl & tc

Marianne Majerus Garden Images 9t, 35l, 36b, 37

Clive Nichols Garden Photography 5l

ILLUSTRATIONS

Lizzie Harper 48, 49, 50, 53a & b, 54a, b & c

Sue Hillier 53c, d & e

Janet Tanner 45

Thanks are also due to the following designers and owners, whose
gardens appear in the book:

Susan Bennett and Earl Hyde 35l; Veronica Clein 33; Carol Klein,
Glebe Cottage, Devon 34b; Christopher Lloyd, Great Dixter, East
Sussex 12, 14b, 16r, 18l, 28, 30t; Dineke Logtenberg, De Boschhoeve,
Holland 32t; John Massey 36t; Clare Matthews 39tl; The National
Trust, Sissinghurst Castle Gardens, Kent 27; Sarah Raven, Perch Hill,
East Sussex 5r, 8, 17r, 24, 31tr; Carol and Malcolm Skinner, Eastgrove
Cottage Garden Nursery, Worcestershire 10; Sue Whittington 37

While every effort has been made to trace and acknowledge all
copyright holders, the publisher would like to apologize should there
be any errors or omissions.